IN PLAIN SIGHT

DEVOTIONAL & GROUP STUDY GUIDE

Understanding and Embracing God's Heart
for the Vulnerable and Broken

by Stacia Freeman
and David Trotter

Foreword by Natalie Grant

Awaken Media

IN PLAIN SIGHT: Devotional and Group Study Guide
by Stacia Freeman and David Trotter

Scripture quotations marked (NIV) are taken from the Holy Bible, New International Version®, NIV®. Copyright © 1973, 1978, 1984, 2011 by Biblica, Inc.™ Used by permission of Zondervan. All rights reserved worldwide. www.zondervan.com The "NIV" and "New International Version" are trademarks registered in the United States Patent and Trademark Office by Biblica, Inc.™

Scripture taken from The Message. Copyright © 1993, 1994, 1995, 1996, 2000, 2001, 2002. Used by permission of NavPress Publishing Group.

Designed by 8TRACKstudios - www.8trackstudios.com

ISBN: 978-1-935798-09-5

To the victims of sex trafficking
who long to experience freedom,
but don't know how to find it.

To the unsung abolitionists
who are fighting for freedom
on behalf of the enslaved.

To the average person
who wants to do something
about it, but doesn't know how.

TABLE OF CONTENTS

TABLE OF CONTENTS

ABOUT : IN PLAIN SIGHT

IN PLAIN SIGHT is a three-part campaign to help stop sex trafficking in the United States. We are focused on educating the American public on a dark problem that is exploding across the nation and motivating people to take action in their own communities.

IN PLAIN SIGHT: Stories of Hope and Freedom

Executive produced and narrated by Natalie Grant, the documentary features six modern-day abolitionists as they fight sex trafficking across America. Journeying to six US cities, the film opens viewer's eyes to what's happening down the street "in plain sight".

IN PLAIN SIGHT: Devotional and Group Study Guide

After watching the film, individuals and faith-based small groups, Bible studies, and Sunday School classes can use the book to understand and embrace God's heart for the vulnerable and broken in our world.

IN PLAIN SIGHT: Songs of Hope and Freedom

To help fund the work of Hope for Justice, an accompanying music album is available for purchase and features hymns recorded by well-known artists who turn our attention to the hope and healing needed to overcome this darkness. Not only is this an album that can be enjoyed on your own, we hope you'll utilize the songs in a time of weekly worship as you gather with your small group (lyrics included in the back of this book).

Website – www.inplainsightfilm.com
Facebook – www.facebook.com/inplainsightfilm
Twitter – www.twitter.com/inplainsightnow

JOIN THE MOVEMENT

1. HOST A SCREENING

For more information on how to host a screening of the IN PLAIN SIGHT documentary in your area, go to **www.inplainsightfilm.com/screening**.

2. SUPPORT AFTERCARE HOMES

To make a donation directly to one of the organizations featured in the documentary, go to **www.inplainsightfilm.com/donate**.

3. SUPPORT THE FILM

To make a tax-deductible donation to Awaken Media and help us spread the film across the world, go to **www.storiesoffreedom.com**.

It was 2004 - the year everything changed for me. I describe it as the year I was wrecked in the best possible way. My comfortable little life as I had known was turned completely upside down.

I learned that slavery still exists in our world.

In fact, I learned there are more slaves in the world today than at any point in history, and a large percentage of the victims are children. Yes, the most innocent among us, are being exploited and ravaged.

Although I heard about sex trafficking on TV and read about it online, I actually saw that this horrific evil was real as I walked the streets of the red-light district in Mumbai. I witnessed first-hand those trapped by the confines of oppression as I saw little children for sale on the street. I walked through a brothel where a young girl of only 15 years of age was forced to work. This was only made worse by the fact that she was also a mother of an 18-month-old baby who she had to tether to the bedpost while she serviced clients so her child wouldn't get lost.

It was the greatest evil I had ever experienced.
Yet, in the midst of the darkness, hope still remained.

I had the opportunity to meet many girls, young girls, rescued from those same streets and given hope through love and authenticity. I will never forget the moment I met a young woman who had been trafficked at the age of 12, rescued at 19, and though we did not speak the same language, she took my hands and whispered one name to me that she knew I would understand.

"Jesus", she said with tears streaming down her cheeks.

In that moment, I saw the restorative power of Christ in a way I had never experienced before. His hope had revived her, and she had light and joy in her eyes in spite of the tragedy and unthinkable events of her past. The same Jesus who prompted me toward this issue had rescued this sweet child, and she knew of His hope and His promise to make all things new.

I was reminded that Light always conquers the dark.

The same power that restored that victim of sex trafficking is the same power that lives in all of us that believe. This encounter forever changed my life, and I resolved to use my voice and platform to tell others about the hope they can offer through His power living within us.

As followers of Christ, we are persuaded to value the oppressed - to pour ourselves into those who are downtrodden. In Psalm 34:18, the Bible specifically reminds us that God is close to the broken-hearted; therefore, we should make ourselves available to them as well. Over the course of my 20 years in Christian music, I have seen many broken people clinging to the promises of God - His promise for provision, forgiveness, and healing. Survivors of sex trafficking and exploitation need our love, and they need us to point them toward a loving Father who takes all things broken, tattered, defunct, and old - and makes them new.

My hope is that your heart will be broken and your eyes will be opened to this issue through the "IN PLAIN SIGHT" devotional and study guide. I pray that you will respond with, "Here I am" and make yourself a beacon of hope and light for the oppressed in this world.

Together we are equipped to end this travesty in our lifetime, and we will stand together and say "no more" to slavery. I, along with all of us at **Hope for Justice**, link arms with you and declare freedom for all those hidden in the darkness who are waiting for rescue - His rescue - made evident through all of us.

Natalie Grant
August 2014
Nashville, Tennessee

HOW TO USE THIS BOOK

Designed to accompany the IN PLAIN SIGHT documentary and music album, this book is both a personal devotional and group study guide. While the topic of sex trafficking has been interwoven through personal stories and points of insight, we have written it in a way to provide viewers of the film with a deeper study of God's heart for the vulnerable and broken.

After watching the documentary within your small group or at a film screening:

→ **Use this as a small group study and daily devotional.**
Encourage group members to read the "Introduction" prior to watching the film, and spend the first session interacting about the documentary by using the discussion questions for "Group Session Week #1".

To facilitate a simple time of worship, we have included the lyrics in the back of this book to the hymns found on the IN PLAIN SIGHT album. Play a couple of the songs and have your group sing along.

Then, after the first group experience, there are six daily devotions for each group member to read and meditate upon in preparation for the next meeting.

→ **Or, just use this as a personal devotional by yourself.**
If you prefer to utilize this book as a personal devotional outside of a group setting, you can simply use the discussion questions found in the Group Sessions as that day's devotional. Although you are processing this material on your own, we encourage you to share what you're learning with friends and family throughout the 31 days.

TELL THE WORLD

As you know, one of the greatest ways we can raise awareness about the epidemic of sex trafficking in America is through social media.

TWEET IT OUT.
Each daily devotion has a "tweetable" quote that you can share on Facebook or Twitter if you like. Tag them #inplainsightfilm.

INSTAGRAM IT.
At the end of each daily devotional, you'll also find an Instagram-ready quote to photograph with your phone and post. Tag them #inplainsightfilm as well.

SEND US YOUR SMALL GROUP PHOTO.
Tell us what you're learning, and send us a photo of your small group (david@inplainsightfilm.com) holding up your books. Don't forget to share what city or church you're from, and we'll post it on the IN PLAIN SIGHT Facebook page!

Several years ago, I first became aware of sex trafficking overseas on a mission trip in India, but I never tied it in with something happening in the United States. For a long time, this was more of a global issue, and it never crossed my mind that there are people in our country who are struggling under the same type of oppression.

As I heard from my friend, Natalie Grant, that this was happening in our country as well, there was a part of me that said, "No way! How is it even possible that's really taking place in the States - even in Nashville?"

In fact, when we were researching a warehouse for one of our church campuses, I came across some related stories online. I found out that a hotel right across the street was the location of several stings - a place where people had been arrested and where prostitutes had been held against their will.

Not only is this happening in the US.
Not only is this happening in the Southeast.
It's happening right across the street from our church.
That was just mind-boggling to me.

It's not alright that there are more slaves in the world today than any other time in human history. It's not okay there are people in Nashville abusing women and children, and we've got to do something about it.

There are millions of people in the world who don't have a voice right now, and we need to step up and be there voice. Any influence we have should be used for people who don't have influence.

(Excerpt from interview with Pete Wilson)

We claim to worship a God that is about freedom. We have an incredible opportunity to bring awareness to our country and really get behind something that I believe our faith compels us to get behind. It's going to take a lot of people partnering together to say, "Enough is enough. This can't happen on our watch. It just can't."

When you turn on the news, it can be heartbreaking. You can almost feel like the hope is being sucked out of you, but the reality is that we have hope. Regardless of the circumstances or darkness in our world, we have a hope that supersedes all of that, and we're called to shine a bright light in a dark world.

Not only are we called to have hope, but we're called to extend hope to the hopeless of our world.

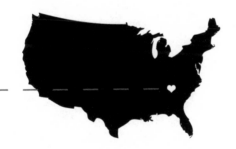

LEADER NOTES - WEEK #1: During your first group session, begin by watching the IN PLAIN SIGHT documentary, and spend the remaining time reflecting on the film with the help of the discussion questions provided. If your group has already seen the film at a screening, use the beginning of your group time to share a meal together, and then use the discussion questions to process what you experienced through the documentary. It is up to you and your group whether you want to review the group questions and write out your answers in preparation for each group session.

Do You Know What's Going On In Your City?

You may not see it, but it's happening…in homes, motels, hotels, truck stops, and spas across America. An estimated 100,000 children - and thousands more women - are being sold for sex in the United States each year. Over 80% of victims are US citizens – not foreign nationals transported into our country, and the average age a victim enters the sex trade is between 12 and 14 years of age.

In the midst of the darkness, eyes are being opened, and people are starting to come to grips with what's happening around them. They're saying, "enough is enough", and powerful women and men are rising up to take on the challenge.

You may think this just happens in cities like LA, New York, or Las Vegas. Think again. Victims have been rescued in all 50 states – in cities, towns, and rural areas. Do you know what's really going on in your city?

WHAT IS SEX TRAFFICKING?

Sex trafficking is a commercial sex act induced by force, fraud, or coercion, or in which the person induced to perform such act has not attained 18 years of age.

Any minor engaged in a commercial sex act is considered a trafficking victim regardless of whether force, fraud, or coercion is involved. In other words, there is no such thing as a child prostitute. He or she is a trafficking victim.

You may be wondering, "How does this even happen in America?" While every victim's story is unique, there is a pattern that seems to emerge as you hear enough stories, and it starts with neglect and sexual abuse at a very young age. Boundaries are crossed, innocence has been stolen, and there's a confusion about what is normal.

The result…a vulnerability that others prey upon.

1. Prior to watching the documentary, how would you describe your knowledge of sex trafficking in the United States?

2. What did you like best about the film, and why?

3. What did you learn from watching the film?

4. Which survivor captured your heart, and why?

5. Is there a particular statement from an abolitionist, law enforcement officer, or expert that stands out to you? Why did it impact you?

6. After watching the film, how did you feel, and why? Hopeful? Angry? Depressed? Overwhelmed? Confused? Determined?

7. Do you believe that sex trafficking is happening in your city? Why or why not? If not, would you be willing to do some research to find out? (Such as calling your local police department, FBI office, or researching online...)

Read Micah 6:8 in the two versions provided below:

"He has shown you, O mortal, what is good. And what does the LORD require of you? To act justly and to love mercy and to walk humbly with your God." (NIV)

"But he's already made it plain how to live, what to do, what GOD is looking for in men and women. It's quite simple: Do what is fair and just to your neighbor, be compassionate and loyal in your love, And don't take yourself too seriously - take God seriously." (MSG)

8. What does this Scripture mean to you in light of what you now know about sex trafficking in your city?

Turn to "31 Ways to Take Action" in the back of the book.
Let's take time to read one action step per person – working our way around the group – until we've read them all.

9. After reading through the possible action steps, which one or two are you personally compelled by? Why?

10. What would it practically look like for you to start to take action this next week? Are you willing to take that step?

11. Is there something that we (as a group) would like to do to take action together?

Leader Note: Choose several people to pray for the items below, or break into smaller groups of 2-3 people.

→ Pray for the victims of sex trafficking in the United States.

→ Pray for the six organizations featured in the film.

Hope for Justice (Stacia Freeman) – Nashville, TN
P.A.T.H. (Louise Allison) – Little Rock, AR
Redeemed (Bobbie Marks) – Houston, TX
Traffick911 (Deena Graves) – Dallas, TX
Courage Worldwide (Jenny Williamson) – Sacramento, CA
The Samaritan Women (Jeanne Allert) – Baltimore, MD

→ Ask for wisdom / motivation on how to take action as a group.

From Condemnation to Compassion

Open your Bible and begin by reading John 8:1-11.
(Feel free to download the YouVersion app or use www.Bible.com.)

We don't know the story of this woman, do we? We know she has been caught in the midst of adultery, but we don't know how or why she's gotten to this place in her life.

Is this a one-time encounter or a pattern in her life?
Was she seduced, or was she the seducer?
Is she addicted to sex or longing for a tender touch?
Or, was she even being forced to have sex with a powerful man?
We just don't know.

How easy it is to assume so much about another person without truly understanding the story of their lives. We seem to have a tendency to focus on the outward acts without having knowledge of a person's situation, don't we? We're not talking about excuses for harmful behavior here. We're talking about developing empathy for others and the painful situation in which they find themselves.

We're talking about a shift from condemnation to compassion.

When the teachers of the law and the Pharisees brought this woman to Jesus, they had no interest in anything other than her act of adultery. They didn't care about her past or even her future. They wanted justice (and to set a trap for Jesus).

With incredible wisdom, Jesus responds, *"Let any one of you who is without sin be the first to throw a stone at her." (John 8:7 – NIV)*

Every person has a story, and every story has a thread of vulnerability and brokenness. For many of us, this thread is hidden behind a thin veneer of wanting to appear put together or successful or a good Christian.

The truth is we are all vulnerable in some way,
and we have *all* experienced brokenness.

None of us have a story that is without disappointment, loneliness, dissolution, regret, letdown, suffering, betrayal, or pain. Some of us have experienced more of this brokenness than others, and we all respond to these experiences differently. Remember the beginning of the film? Hope (as we call her) says...

> *"I didn't grow up in a family. I didn't have a chance like everybody else did. I didn't have a roof and...like I said, I was eight years old and the next thing I knew I was having sex for money and then I started crying and I got addicted to something, and it made me feel better and I didn't have to be in that position. So, I hate when people judge us, because you never know where you can be just because I'm out here and doing what I'm doing...that doesn't mean that you never know where you could have been. My, my hand got dealt different than everybody else's hand did...you know? Don't judge a person. Get to know'em."*

There are vulnerable and broken people everywhere...
even when you look in the mirror.

💡 TIME TO REFLECT

1. In what ways do you sense that you are vulnerable?

- ☐ Bad habits
- ☐ Fearful of something
- ☐ Prone to depression
- ☐ Learning disability
- ☐ Addictions
- ☐ Struggle with anxiety
- ☐ Physical handicap
- ☐ Ongoing illness

2. In what ways have you experienced brokenness?

- ☐ Disappointment
- ☐ Dissolution
- ☐ Letdown
- ☐ Betrayal
- ☐ Loneliness
- ☐ Regret
- ☐ Suffering
- ☐ Pain

3. When people have ignored or condemned you in the midst of a challenging situation, did you find it hurtful? Why or why not?

🛜 PRAYER

"Jesus, thank you for your compassion in my life. Thank you for not condemning me when I made decisions that were hurtful to others and myself. Help me to develop that same compassion for the people in my life and my city who are vulnerable and broken."

🐦 QUOTE OF THE DAY

"My hand got dealt different than everybody else's hand did...
you know? Don't judge a person. Get to know'em."
Hope #inplainsightfilm

📷 INSTAGRAM IT!

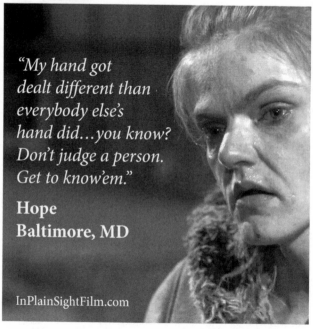

"My hand got dealt different than everybody else's hand did...you know? Don't judge a person. Get to know'em."

Hope
Baltimore, MD

InPlainSightFilm.com

Take a photo with your phone and post on Instagram!

We're All Connected.

Let's begin by reading John 4:1-26.
(YouVersion app or www.Bible.com)

This is quite a conversation around what amounts to be an ancient-day water cooler as Jesus breaks all sorts of societal norms by speaking with this woman at the well.

Why is this Jew associating with a Samaritan…a half-breed?
Why is this man speaking to a woman…outside of his family?
And, why is this woman going to draw water at the hottest point in the day…at noon?

Perhaps, it's because the other women have ostracized her due to five failed marriages and the fact that she's now living with a new man. By crossing these barriers and asking the woman for a drink of water, Jesus is outwardly demonstrating an inward reality.

The reality is that we are all connected as human beings, because we have been created in the image of God. Every single one of us. God created and loves us…equally. We are connected within the fabric of this world…as brothers and sisters.

Even though we allow the color of our skin, the amount in our bank account, the education we've earned (or haven't), and the language we speak to create external barriers that separate, we are all connected at a deep level.

Jesus knows this, and he's willing to cross all those barriers to demonstrate love.

Not only does he interact with the Samaritan woman, but he also enters into a spiritual conversation of great depth. Ultimately, he reveals to her that he is the Messiah – something he wasn't shouting out to the rest of the world. Why would Jesus reveal his identity to a woman of ill repute?

→ He is making her value known as a human being.

→ He is showing her that she is worth any hassle he might get from someone looking on.

→ He is demonstrating the inward reality that we are all connected on this Earth.

When we see someone who is suffering in some way, it's easy to allow the earthly barriers to prevent us from acknowledging the fact that we're all connected. When we turn our heads to ignore the suffering of another, it is a sign we are disconnected – not only from that person but also from ourselves. Why? Because we're meant to be connected to one another. When we care for another human being, it's a sign that we are connected to all of humanity. We are demonstrating outwardly the inward reality of our connectedness.

In the film, you may remember when Jenny Williamson, founder of Courage Worldwide (Sacramento, CA), says...

> "The Lord reminded me that I always wanted daughters, and I thought I'm too old to have those kids. He said, 'Your kids are being raped, abused, and tortured on the streets. Those are your daughters.' In that moment in my heart got deposited this love for kids I didn't know...the daughters I always wanted."

She was coming to grips with the reality of her connectedness to those girls who were (and are) suffering at the hands of traffickers. With the recognition of our connection to one another, there is an opportunity to extend compassion and ultimately to take action.

💡 TIME TO REFLECT

1. **Do you think Jesus was taking a chance by having a conversation with the Samaritan woman? Why or why not?**

2. **Are there certain groups of people you ostracize or disconnect from by criticizing them in your mind (or through your words)?**

3. What would you be risking if you started to connect with those people in a positive way?

 **PRAYER**

"Jesus, give me eyes to see how I'm connected to all of humanity. Help me to see each person as your beautiful, unique creation who you love and cherish. Give me opportunities today to connect with people I wouldn't normally connect with. I'll be looking for who you bring my way."

 **QUOTE OF THE DAY**

"It really boils down to this: that all life is interrelated...
Whatever affects one directly, affects all indirectly."
Martin Luther King, Jr. #inplainsightfilm

INSTAGRAM IT!

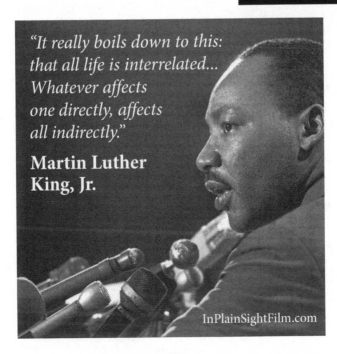

"It really boils down to this: that all life is interrelated... Whatever affects one directly, affects all indirectly."
Martin Luther King, Jr.

InPlainSightFilm.com

Looking Down or Looking Up?

Let's begin by reading Luke 7:36-50.
(YouVersion app or www.Bible.com)

Once again, Jesus is pushing social boundaries while he's surrounded by a group of Pharisees, powerful religious separatists devoted to the Law in extreme ways. While Jesus was reclining at the table for dinner, a "sinful" woman heard about his presence, and she walks into the home with a jar of perfume.

Verse 38 says, *"As she stood behind him at his feet weeping, she began to wet his feet with her tears. Then she wiped them with her hair, kissed them and poured perfume on them."* (NIV)

While this sounds like a ludicrous encounter in our culture, it would have been seen as highly seductive to the Pharisees as they look through the lens of her current lifestyle.

Many scholars believe that this woman is a prostitute, and everyone in town knows about it. Rubbing perfume all over someone with her hair would have been a sensual encounter in most instances, but in this moment, Jesus knows that it is an act of honor and even worship.

The Pharisees are confronted with the reality of their hearts. There is disdain for this woman – a sinner – who is invading their party and making a scene with Jesus.

Yet, Jesus loves her.
And, Jesus allows her to love him.

The tears that flow down her cheeks are tears of desperation – a longing for a new way of life. We don't know her full story, but we do know that the Pharisees (and probably many others) looked down upon her. What a toll this takes on the human spirit!

Jesus takes this moment to address Simon, his host..."*Do you see this woman? I came into your house. You did not give me any water for my feet, but she wet my feet with her tears and wiped them with her hair. You did not give me a kiss, but this woman, from the time I entered, has not stopped kissing my feet. You did not put oil on my head, but she has poured perfume on my feet. Therefore, I tell you, her many sins have been forgiven—as her great love has shown. But whoever has been forgiven little loves little.*" *(Luke 4:44-47 – NIV)*

In other words, this woman knows that she needs forgiveness and grace in large portion, and she is displaying her love and appreciation for Jesus in great measure. In that moment, she didn't choose to cover up her problems and put on a "happy face". She was desperate for forgiveness and life transformation, and she was willing to do something dramatic to get it. Notice the Pharisees are looking *down* on the woman, while she is looking *up* at Jesus – thankful for his forgiveness. Do you see the difference in posture between the two?

Where do you want to be looking? *Down* upon people who are struggling or sinful or "less than" in some way? Or, looking *up* at Jesus... recognizing your own need for forgiveness right alongside this woman?

Looking down on people (judging them) because of their situation is so easy to do, isn't it? Whether it's calling them a name in our heads as we drive by or muttering words of displeasure as we read a news story, we often pronounce judgments on that person – preventing us from seeing them as a human being loved by God. Even in our effort to help people in need, it's easy to think we're the ones who are helping "those people."

What if we recognized that we are "one of them"? We are no different than that "sinful woman" in the fact that we're all vulnerable to sin, and we're all broken and hurting in some way. What if we started looking up at Jesus rather than down on others?

💡 TIME TO REFLECT

1. **Why do you think we have a tendency to look down on people who are struggling?**

2. If you walked into a dinner party with Jesus as a guest, do you think you'd be more like the Pharisees or more like the woman? Why?

"Jesus, help me to recognize that I'm no better than this woman, and I have many things in common with her. Help me to stop looking down on people who are different than me and start looking up at you as my example. I want to be more like you."

🐦 QUOTE OF THE DAY

"True humility is not thinking less of yourself;
it is thinking of yourself less." **C.S. Lewis**
#inplainsightfilm

📷 INSTAGRAM IT!

InPlainSightFilm.com

"True humility is not thinking less of yourself; it is thinking of yourself less."
C.S. Lewis

A BEAUTIFUL HOME

JESSICA, Survivor of Sex Traficking
Traffick911 - Dallas, TX

When I was just 10 years old, my Mom's boyfriend started abusing me. "Just hush, and please don't tell," he would say to me. I never felt safe in my own home, and after months of abuse, I just couldn't take it anymore.

At 11, I ran away from home, and a gang offered me an initial refuge that soon turned into another nightmare. They started selling me to other gangs for drugs, and I lived with the horror of being raped and beaten repeatedly for years. I was just a young, little girl who felt all alone and wanted to go home.

At 16, I was placed in juvenile detention, and Traffick911 came and talked to us about the "Traps of a Trafficker", and I told them my story.

Home. Home. Home. I never really had one.
Why? Because the people I loved the most betrayed me.

Every time I would get scared, I would want to run back home...but I had no place to go. Without a family, I hated watching others go home to sleep and rest. If it wasn't for that man and for the gang, I would have loved home, but that was nothing more than a fairytale story in my head.

Traffick911 introduced me to Jesus, and everything started changing. After they heard my story, they convinced a judge to let me go live at their home for girls. Not only did God give me a beautiful family, but I finally was able to experience a true "home".

Somewhere I could run to.
Somewhere I could rest and sleep.
Somewhere I didn't have to be afraid of the next knock on the door.

Thank you for giving me the home I always wanted.

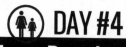

DAY #4
Love People and Use Things

Let's begin by reading Psalm 139:13-16.
(YouVersion app or www.Bible.com)

Think back to your early years when you got your first skateboard or bike. You loved it, didn't you? Maybe you dreamed about it for months or even years before finally getting one. Once you paid for it or someone gave it to you as a gift, you probably spent all sorts of time riding it all over the place. Maybe you spent even more money upgrading it and then showing it off to friends. You finally owned it, and it was designed to serve you. It was all yours!

You didn't want it to break or fall apart, so you maintained it for the sole purpose of ensuring it would still function when you were ready to ride. Yet, when it got too old or "used up", you probably put it up for sale or even tossed it in the trash. This is how we treat objects, because they are meant to be owned and used. Unfortunately, we often treat people in the same way. We turn people into "things" when we...

→ Envision a person as a sexual object.
→ View a person purely based on looks or external appearance.
→ Treat a person as a tool to be used for our own pleasure or purpose.
→ Act as if a person is silent - lacking the capacity to speak.
→ Assume a person's experiences or feelings aren't important.

The objectification of people is not limited to viewing or treating women as a sexual object, although that is one of the most common ways in which it plays out.

Remember what David said, *"You have searched me, Lord, and you know me. You know when I sit and when I rise; you perceive my thoughts from afar." (Psalm 139:1-2 – NIV)* This tells us that our thoughts are important to God. Why? Because our thoughts ultimately result in our words and behaviors. How we think will ultimately determine how we live.

Consider all the ways in which we treat people as objects to be used for our own pleasure or purpose. Have you ever treated a waiter, car wash attendant, landscaper, post office worker, or nurse as something less than a human being created by God? We probably all have. While objects are to be owned and used, people are to be honored and cherished.

The reason is very simple – God created humankind "in His image" giving us far greater value than any other creation. The Bible tells us we are God's handiwork, and every person on this planet has been given a spirit that will last way beyond the 80+ years we live in our Earth-suit.

Remember what David wrote, *"For you created my inmost being; you knit me together in my mother's womb. I praise you because I am fearfully and wonderfully made..." (Psalm 139:13-14 – NIV)*

When you see the gorgeous guy walking down the street or when you look at the beautifully Photoshopped woman in the advertisement, he or she was fearfully and wonderfully made by God, and that person is incredibly valuable in the eyes of our Father. No matter what our culture says or how an advertising agency is using them or even how he or she is dressed, that person is more than the composite of their external appearance.

God says to Samuel, *"The Lord does not look at the things people look at. People look at the outward appearance, but the Lord looks at the heart." (1 Samuel 16:7 – NIV)*

Every person had a mother and a father, and they've experienced the ups and downs of life. Every person has a story, and they have hopes, dreams, and fears...just like you and me.

💡 TIME TO REFLECT

1. **Put yourself in the position of someone you have objectified recently. Would you want someone treating you the same way? Why or why not?**

2. Over the next 24 hours as you see people and connect with them, would you be willing to ask yourself, "Am I treating him or her like an object or a person?"

🛜 PRAYER

"Jesus, help me to be aware of the times when I am objectifying another human being. Give me eyes to see every single person as your precious creation. I want to honor and cherish people by the way I think and talk about them."

🐦 QUOTE OF THE DAY

"What most people need to learn in life is how to love people and use things instead of using people and loving things."
Zelda Fitzgerald #inplainsightfilm

📷 INSTAGRAM IT!

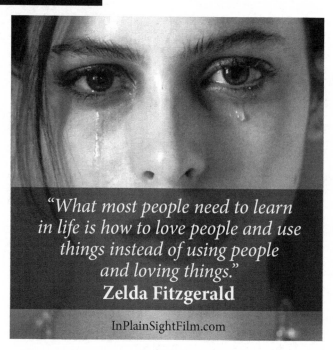

"What most people need to learn in life is how to love people and use things instead of using people and loving things."
Zelda Fitzgerald

InPlainSightFilm.com

Sensitive in the Midst of Chaos

Let's begin by reading Mark 5:21-34.
(YouVersion app or www.Bible.com)

As Jesus is on his way to heal a little girl who is dying, a large crowd is pressing around him. Can you imagine the throng of people wanting to get close to this man who has been healing people and teaching about a new way of life?

As many are jockeying for position, there is a woman who is looking for more than a glimpse of this travelling rabbi. She was desperate for a touch.

"Subject to bleeding for 12 years," Mark tells us.

Ask any woman what that would be like, and she'll probably shake her head in disbelief. Without any of the modern conveniences women are currently accustomed to, this woman had to deal with this bleeding on a daily basis, and there wasn't a single doctor who could help her.

Yet, she knows that Jesus can… *"If I just touch his clothes, I will be healed."*

As she works her way through the crowd, she reaches out to touch his garment, and she is instantly healed. If that isn't amazing enough, Jesus actually recognizes that power had gone out from him.

Jesus was sensitive to her plight.

People were probably shouting his name, calling for his attention, and grabbing his hands – all while he was being led to the home of a dying girl. Yet, he was sensitive to the one who reached out to him in desperation.

In the chaos of life, we have an abundance of things calling out for our attention these days, and it's easy to tune out the voices of those who are vulnerable and broken. We avoid their touch by turning the channel, driving around that part of town, or dodging people in need (even close friends).

While some of us are naturally sensitive, others of us have an opportunity to be more aware of those in our city who are troubled and suffering.

When interacting with your co-workers, the guy who mows your lawn, a waiter/waitress, or the person who is asking you for money, how sensitive are you to their plight? Almost everyone we come in contact with has a challenge they are walking through at this very moment in life. Something is troubling them, and we have the opportunity to be sensitive.

Not only was the woman healed instantly, but Jesus says to her, *"Daughter, your faith has healed you. Go in peace and be freed from your suffering." (v. 34)*

Can you imagine the look on her face and the bounce in her step? Her life was changed forever because of the power of Jesus and his sensitivity to her brokenness. Is it possible that God might want to use you to bring hope and healing to people who are suffering in your city? Could it be that He may want to use your gifts to free women and children from the horrific suffering of being sold for sex?

♀ TIME TO REFLECT

1. **What prevents you from being more sensitive to the needs of troubled people in your city?**

2. **What practical steps could you take to increase your sensitivity? Researching a problem in-depth or developing a relationship with someone who is wrestling with that issue?**

3. Would you be willing to ask three people you come in contact with today, "How are you?"…and really mean it…and listen?

PRAYER

"Jesus, help me to be sensitive to the needs of people within my community. Open my heart to the plight of people who are struggling, and give me eyes to see practical ways I can make a difference. Give me the courage to tune in rather than tuning out."

QUOTE OF THE DAY

"Be kind,
for everyone you meet is fighting a hard battle."
Ian MacLaren #inplainsightfilm

INSTAGRAM IT!

(👫) DAY #6
Do You Want to Get Well?

Let's begin by reading John 5:1-15.
(YouVersion app or www.Bible.com)

This man has been unable to walk for 38 years, and he's hanging out with other disabled men and women waiting for an angel to come stir the waters. They believed that whoever got into the water while it was being stirred would be supernaturally healed.

Jesus simply asks, *"Do you want to get well?"*

That's a question we've all probably asked when coming face to face with someone who has been in a challenging situation for a long time. It's as though he or she has become accustomed to being sick or in debt or jobless or addicted or victimized. My guess is that Jesus saw that tendency in this man's life, but Jesus didn't turn away.

I wonder how often we answer that question for people without giving them a chance to respond.

"No, they don't want to get well. They don't want to get clean, seek counseling, develop life skills, or hold down a job. They're too far gone."

In that moment, we're making an assumption about a person's life, and we never even give them the chance to answer the question that Jesus poses.

"Do you want to get well?"

Honestly, in the world of sex trafficking recovery and rehabilitation, there are many ladies who have such a strong "chain around the brain" that they don't even think another life is possible. In fact, it's "normal" to be addicted, sold for sex, and even raped. As one victim said, "I'd rather have sex with a stranger every night than my own father."

There's a sense that things are bad, and nothing is every going to change. It takes someone to ask, "Do you want to get well?" It takes someone who truly cares…someone who has the willingness to be a bridge to the resources that person truly needs. You won't have all the answers or skills, but God will provide people who do.

Frankly, it would be a mistake to think that you and I are not in this same situation as well. For just a moment, think about an area of your own life where *you* are stuck.

Is there something you've given up on? A bad habit, an addiction, a broken relationship, a long-held resentment? Have you become accustomed to the pain and now just assume that it will be there for a lifetime? Perhaps, we should ask ourselves, "Do I want to become well?"

What's holding me back from embracing the love, grace, hope, and forgiveness available to me through Jesus? Once more, we're in a position to realize that we can become "stuck" in some way that's not much different than the people we seek to help. Is there a "chain around your brain" about the issue you're wrestling with?

There are rarely chains holding down a woman or child who is being trafficked. It's usually a chain of coercion and manipulation that prevents them from simply walking away and getting help. We, too, can develop a chain that stops us from getting the help we need, because we think something is impossible to overcome or it will never work out.

Jesus says to us, *"Do you want to get well?"*

💡 TIME TO REFLECT

1. Why is it oftentimes easier to stay stuck than to seek wholeness?

2. Where do you sense you are stuck in life? What's preventing you from saying "yes" to Jesus' offer of help?

3. When you encounter someone who has been stuck for awhile, would you be willing to stop assuming they want to remain stuck? If so, how?

PRAYER 🛜

"Jesus, help me see the places in my own life where I am stuck. I need your power to break those chains around my brain preventing me from moving forward. You are my source of hope and healing, and I invite you to use me in the lives of other people who are stuck."

QUOTE OF THE DAY 🐦

"For some slaves, the first step out of bondage is to learn to see their lives with new eyes." **Kevin Bales #inplainsightfilm**

INSTAGRAM IT! 📷

"For some slaves, the first step out of bondage is to learn to see their lives with new eyes."

Kevin Bales

InPlainSightFilm.com

BELIEVE IN ME

LIZ, Survivor of Sex Traficking
Courage Worldwide - Sacramento, CA

When I was 6 years old, my family began selling me to men, and I was photographed for pornography as early as I can remember. I wanted to be free, to be safe, and to be loved. I wanted a family.

My day to day existence was defined by the hours men would enter and leave my bedroom. My life was dark and confusing for years, and there was no hope to be found. I just wanted someone to leave my bedroom door open so I could escape. I believed the lies that this was all I was good at. I stopped hoping to be rescued, because I didn't think it was even possible.

One day, as an adult, I was looking online and came across a music video called "Believe In Me" - made by a woman (Jenny Williamson) who had a dream to build homes for girls. Tears began to fall down my face, because I wanted someone to believe in *me*. I sent her email, and that's when my story began to change. Her love and encouragement helped me to walk away from the darkness that had defined my life. It was terrifying to leave, but I didn't want to keep living that way.

My life *is* worth living, and I believe it with everything in me.

Walking away was the hardest and most rewarding act I have ever done. It has been four years since I moved to California and began to be called "family" by people I didn't even know at the time. Jenny and her family adopted me even though I wasn't a young girl anymore, and they helped me see I am worthy of love and value. I now help and mentor other girls, some who are at Courage House, because I want them to know they are not invisible like I believed so long ago.

I am now using my freedom to help others be set free.

We've provided a simple "flow" for you to walk through with the group. Follow the readings and questions – giving each member an opportunity to share as they wish.

Prepare to utilize the IN PLAIN SIGHT music album with a CD or mp3 player for a time of worship with your group (lyrics in the back of this book).

 BELONG

Take time to go around the group sharing something that impacted you from the last six days of devotional reading. Be sure to share your name if you've just started meeting or if there's someone relatively new in the group.

What inspired or challenged you?

CELEBRATE

Let's begin by taking some time quiet our hearts and focus our minds. Turn to the back of this book to sing along with these two hymns. Don't worry about what your voice sounds like. Just sing to God. Before beginning, let's take a moment to pray and ask God to remind us of these timeless truths as we worship Him.

"In Christ Alone" – Natalie Grant
"It Is Well" – Jeremy Camp

📄 GROW

We need to be honest that emotionalism often drives our response to atrocities like sex trafficking. Whether we're completely overwhelmed and choose to bury our heads in the sand or we're devastated by this reality and choose to respond out of guilt, we're better off addressing this issue out of the depth of our faith - rather than just our emotions.

Think about the Grand Story we're living in as human beings.

God created us to be in relationship with Him, and we were designed to experience a life of freedom with access to all the love, hope, and joy we would ever need. Unfortunately, our ancient ancestors (Adam and Eve) turned their backs on Him in an effort to blaze their own trail through life. The world-altering result...a sin existence we all have inherited. From that moment in the Garden of Eden, there has been a cosmic battle between the forces of good and evil, and we're in the midst of it.

→ Every human being longs for meaning, purpose, love, and freedom.
→ Forces of darkness seek to prevent us from experiencing the goodness that God designed for us.
→ God sent Jesus as His representative to demonstrate His undying love, rescue us from darkness, and give us the freedom we were originally intended to experience.

If you haven't noticed, this is the most popular storyline you see in literature and movies – a hero, a villain, and the object of the hero's affection. That's because it is *the Story* we're all living.

Here's the truth - sex trafficking is one of the most heinous tools every devised by the Evil One to prevent us from experiencing the freedom we were all designed for.

Let's begin by reading Romans 6:6-14 in The Message:

"Could it be any clearer? Our old way of life was nailed to the cross with Christ, a decisive end to that sin-miserable life—no longer at sin's every beck and call! What we believe is this: If we get included in Christ's sin-conquering death, we also get included in his life-saving resurrection.

We know that when Jesus was raised from the dead it was a signal of the end of death-as-the-end. Never again will death have the last word. When Jesus died, he took sin down with him, but alive he brings God down to us. From now on, think of it this way: Sin speaks a dead language that means nothing to you; God speaks your mother tongue, and you hang on every word. You are dead to sin and alive to God. That's what Jesus did.

That means you must not give sin a vote in the way you conduct your lives. Don't give it the time of day. Don't even run little errands that are connected with that old way of life. Throw yourselves wholeheartedly and full-time—remember, you've been raised from the dead!—into God's way of doing things. Sin can't tell you how to live. After all, you're not living under that old tyranny any longer. You're living in the freedom of God."

1. **If you set aside how you used to describe sin and simply look at this passage, how would you describe what "sin" does to us?**

2. **Paul writes, "Sin speaks a dead language that means nothing to you; God speaks your mother tongue, and you hang on every word." Play with the differences between this dead language and our mother tongue. What's the big difference?**

3. **While an eternity with God is the greatest gift of all, what are the benefits of "living in the freedom of God"?**

Let's continue reading Romans 6:15-23 in The Message:

"So, since we're out from under the old tyranny, does that mean we can live any old way we want? Since we're free in the freedom of God, can we do anything that comes to mind? Hardly. You know well enough from your own experience that there are some acts of so-called freedom that destroy freedom. Offer yourselves to sin,

for instance, and it's your last free act. But offer yourselves to the ways of God and the freedom never quits. All your lives you've let sin tell you what to do. But thank God you've started listening to a new master, one whose commands set you free to live openly in his freedom!

I'm using this freedom language because it's easy to picture. You can readily recall, can't you, how at one time the more you did just what you felt like doing—not caring about others, not caring about God—the worse your life became and the less freedom you had? And how much different is it now as you live in God's freedom, your lives healed and expansive in holiness?

As long as you did what you felt like doing, ignoring God, you didn't have to bother with right thinking or right living, or right anything for that matter. But do you call that a free life? What did you get out of it? Nothing you're proud of now. Where did it get you? A dead end.

But now that you've found you don't have to listen to sin tell you what to do, and have discovered the delight of listening to God telling you, what a surprise! A whole, healed, put-together life right now, with more and more of life on the way! Work hard for sin your whole life and your pension is death. But God's gift is real life, eternal life, delivered by Jesus, our Master."

4. **One of the first things a pimp (or trafficker) does when "grooming" a victim is to take away his or her freedom. The trafficker makes the victim feel like there are no other options, and they're stuck. In many ways, the victim is a "slave" to the trafficker who uses a "chain around the brain" to control the child or woman.**

   How is that similar to what sin does in our lives?

5. If you envisioned Jesus as your Master (or Leader), how do you think he would treat you? What would he expect from you?

6. When the average person thinks about Christianity, does this type of freedom (as Paul describes it) come to mind? Why or why not?

7. How can you start to experience more of this freedom in your own life? What would that practically look like?

8. Think about the people involved in sex trafficking and their need for true freedom:

   → **Johns** – freedom from the addiction to sex and freedom to have genuine relationships.
   → **Pimps** – freedom from the need to control others and freedom to make a genuine living.
   → **Victims** – freedom from being controlled by others and freedom to experience genuine love.

   As you think about your own life, what do you need freedom from? If you had freedom in that area, how would things be different?

9. What's preventing you from having that type of freedom right now?

SERVE ⚙

Many people who find themselves in a vulnerable or broken place in life are lacking freedom. Something (or someone) has caused them to believe their options are limited to their current existence.

As you go about your week, what if you shared some of your "freedom" with other people? What would it look like to help others open their eyes to new possibilities in their life?

PRAYER 📶

Leader Note: Choose several people to pray for the items below, or break into smaller groups of 2-3 people.

→ Ask God to help you experience true freedom where you need it.

→ Ask God to open your eyes to vulnerable and broken people who are already in your life.

→ Pray for the survivors at the aftercare homes featured in the film – asking God to give them peace, heal their pain, and fill their minds with new thoughts and memories.

Embracing Freedom for Yourself

Last week, we looked at several passages focusing on Jesus' outlook on people – especially the vulnerable and broken. People are not something to be used, fixed, or solved. Each one has a unique story, and God loves all of us equally.

As followers of Jesus, we have the opportunity to connect with God freely and enjoy all the elements of life He originally intended for us to experience. It's not just a new way of life…it's a returning to how life was intended to be lived.

Let's read 2 Corinthians 5:17-21 in The Message…

> "The old life is gone; a new life burgeons! Look at it! All this comes from the God who settled the relationship between us and him, and then called us to settle our relationships with each other. God put the world square with himself through the Messiah, giving the world a fresh start by offering forgiveness of sins. God has given us the task of telling everyone what he is doing. We're Christ's representatives. God uses us to persuade men and women to drop their differences and enter into God's work of making things right between them. We're speaking for Christ himself now: Become friends with God; he's already a friend with you."

Paul is saying…as a follower of Jesus, we get to represent God on this earth. We've been given the task of helping people connect with Him and connect with one another.

You may be thinking, "Wow! Some days, it feels like I'm just trying to make it through my to-do list and collapse into bed. Now I'm being asked to represent God? Yikes!"

Once again, not a burden…but a freedom.
Not a "have to"…but a "get to."

If God's love, acceptance, healing power, wisdom, peace, and hope are *truly* available to us, then our part is simply embracing Him into our lives. This isn't a one-time experience, but a daily openness to what He has for us. God gives us a fresh start (new life), and we can draw upon this freedom every day.

Here's where the adventure begins.

We have an opportunity to tell the world (including the vulnerable and broken) that we don't have to suck it up and keep living a life of survival. There's no need to feel like we're just living for the weekend or the one or two weeks of vacation we squeeze out of the year.

Yet, I'm not sure it's even possible to share something you don't already have yourself. Or, maybe you have it, but you haven't embraced it. Maybe you're not aware of it. Perhaps you need to spend time cultivating an awareness of the freedom available to you as a follower of Jesus.

Remember that we're loved deeply by God,
He has an amazing plan for us,
and we're free to live a remarkable life.
It's easy to forget, isn't it?

As you're reminding yourself of the big God Story we're all living, what if you started to share some of that with others? What if you started sharing… *"Become friends with God; he's already a friend with you."*

💡 TIME TO REFLECT

1. In what area(s) of your life are you prone to feeling stuck? (relationship, vocation, physical health, anger, resentments, etc.)

2. How can you embrace the freedom God has for you in that area of your life? What would that look like?

3. **How could you begin to daily draw upon the resources God has made available to you?**

 **PRAYER**

"Jesus, I want to be your representative, but I first need to be your friend. Help me know how to embrace this new life you have for me, and give me the wisdom to know how and when to share it with others. Thank you for making me free."

 **QUOTE OF THE DAY**

"Love does not claim possession, but gives freedom."
Rabindranath Tagore #inplainsightfilm

INSTAGRAM IT!

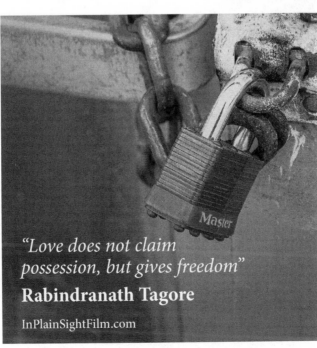

Take a photo with your phone and post on Instagram!

What Do You Need Freedom From?

Freedom is not just a feeling; it is a reality we can live within. If you open up the New Oxford American Dictionary, it is defined as "the power or right to act, speak, or think as one wants without hindrance or restraint."

As followers of Jesus, we have the power and right to be free from things that hold us back from the life God intended for us to live. All of those "things" are tools of the Evil One to prevent us from not only experiencing freedom and also prevent us from sharing that freedom with others who are vulnerable and broken.

Jesus describes the Evil One this way…*"The thief comes only to steal and kill and destroy; I have come that they may have life, and have it to the full." (John 10:10 – NIV)*

Don't you love the idea of having the type of "full life" Jesus is talking about? The challenge is there are quite a few things that can steal, kill, and destroy us in this life. In the passage we're about to read, the apostle Paul warns us about using our freedom to do whatever we want. (As you may have noticed, we like to utilize The Message from time to time, because the modern-day wording can cause the Scriptures to work their way into our hearts in a new way.)

Let's read Galatians 5:19-21 in The Message:

"It is obvious what kind of life develops out of trying to get your own way all the time: repetitive, loveless, cheap sex; a stinking accumulation of mental and emotional garbage; frenzied and joyless grabs for happiness; trinket gods; magic-show religion; paranoid loneliness; cutthroat competition; all-consuming-yet-never-satisfied wants; a brutal temper; an impotence to love or be loved; divided homes and divided lives; small-minded and lopsided pursuits; the vicious habit of depersonalizing everyone into a rival; uncontrolled and uncontrollable addictions; ugly parodies of community. I could

go on. This isn't the first time I have warned you, you know. If you use your freedom this way, you will not inherit God's kingdom."

Isn't this all the stuff we want freedom from?

Sure, a lot of this can feel really good in the moment, but what about when the thin veneer of ecstasy wears off? What about when you finish the gossipy conversation? What about when your rage dissipates? What about when you look at your exorbitant credit card statement? What about the next morning?

Not only does Jesus demonstrate a new way of life,
but the Holy Spirit gives us the power to experience it.

How? Because *"the Spirit of him who raised Jesus from the dead is living in you." (Romans 8:11 – NIV)*

With the Holy Spirit living within us, this new way of life opens up so many possibilities that weren't available to us before. Instead of being stuck in a dead-end life – thinking our options are limited, our eyes are opened to see the Story we're living in and how we get to participate within it.

We don't have to give in to addiction to cope with stress and anxiety.
We don't need to allow anger and resentment to rule our lives.
We don't have to say 'yes' to immediate gratification at the cost of our future.

We can have freedom from so many things that will ultimately steal, kill, and destroy the full life we have been given by Jesus.

 **TIME TO REFLECT**

1. **When Jesus talks about giving you a "full life", what does that mean to you?**

2. What attitude or behavior would you walk away from right now if you could? What's holding you back?

PRAYER 📶

"Jesus, thank you for being a loving Leader who wants me to have a full life. Help me to see the attitudes and behaviors that are holding me back, and give me the courage to allow you to transform me. I want to experience freedom from anything preventing a full and lasting life."

QUOTE OF THE DAY 🐦

"Freedom consists not in doing what we like, but in having the right to do what we ought." **Pope John Paul II #inplainsightfilm**

INSTAGRAM IT! 📷

"Freedom consists not in doing what we like, but in having the right to do what we ought."

Pope John Paul II

InPlainSightFilm.com

Freedom to Do What?

If you've ever tried to change your diet, you know it's nearly impossible to resist certain types of food without replacing them with something healthier. If you simply focus on words like "stop, quit, and resist", you'll probably just go back to eating as much unhealthy stuff as before.

The same thing is true when it comes to having freedom from negative thoughts, attitudes, and behaviors. If we just focus on "stopping", our brains will still be focused on the very thing we're trying to avoid.

Instead of thinking about all the things you want freedom from, what if you focused on all the things you have the freedom to experience?

Let's read Galatians 5:21-26 in The Message:

"But what happens when we live God's way? He brings gifts into our lives, much the same way that fruit appears in an orchard— things like affection for others, exuberance about life, serenity. We develop a willingness to stick with things, a sense of compassion in the heart, and a conviction that a basic holiness permeates things and people. We find ourselves involved in loyal commitments, not needing to force our way in life, able to marshal and direct our energies wisely.

Legalism is helpless in bringing this about; it only gets in the way. Among those who belong to Christ, everything connected with getting our own way and mindlessly responding to what everyone else calls necessities is killed off for good—crucified. Since this is the kind of life we have chosen, the life of the Spirit, let us make sure that we do not just hold it as an idea in our heads or a sentiment in our hearts, but work out its implications in every detail of our lives. That means we will not compare ourselves with each other as if one of us were better and another worse. We have far more interesting things to do with our lives. Each of us is an original."

My guess is we all want these "fruits" in our lives, don't we? Who doesn't want to experience a genuine affection for others, exuberance about life, and serenity? Ironically, these are the very same things we're pursuing when we're led astray by many of our coping mechanisms (overeating, overshopping, overspending, oversexing).

Following Jesus and allowing him to develop these new "fruits" in our life happens from the inside out, and he promises to lead us toward the authentic version of what we've been longing for.

Freedom from...getting our own way (cheap substitutes).
Freedom to...get what we were designed for (authentic version).

Notice the passage says, *"Let us make sure that we do not just hold it as an idea in our heads or a sentiment in our hearts, but work out its implications in every detail of our lives."*

If freedom is just an intellectual idea or a goose bump emotion, we lose out on the practicality of being free. Think about how this freedom can be experienced in the everydayness of your life.

→ Freedom from anger...to forgive.
→ Freedom from anxiety...to be at peace.
→ Freedom from fears...to be courageous.
→ Freedom from depression...to experience joy.
→ Freedom from self-centeredness...to serve others.
→ Freedom from addictions...to be sober and clear-minded.
→ Freedom from comparing ourselves to others...to be the unique person God created you to be.

Now we're talking! This is the type of freedom everyone needs.

💡 TIME TO REFLECT

1. After reading The Message version of Galatians 5, what fruit of the Spirit do you long to experience in your own life?

2. If you were to have a personal conversation with Paul (the author of Galatians), how would he encourage you to cultivate these fruits in your life?

 **PRAYER**

"Jesus, help me to embrace your freedom in my life. Help me feel free to be the person you created me to be and develop the fruits of the Spirit in my life. I want more love, joy, peace, forbearance, kindness, goodness, faithfulness, gentleness, and self-control in my life. I submit myself to you as my Leader, and I invite you to develop these qualities within me."

 **QUOTE OF THE DAY**

"Those who deny freedom to others deserve it not for themselves."
Abraham Lincoln #inplainsightfilm

 **INSTAGRAM IT!**

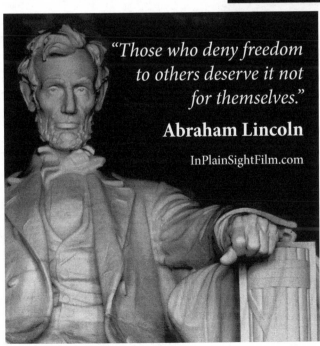

I have always been confused. From an early age, I was forced to watch porn with my mom and her girlfriend, and they would have sex afterwards. When I was 13 years old, my mom committed suicide, and my step-dad went to prison right after for crimes he'd committed.

I was alone, but somehow felt relieved from all the screaming, beatings, and chaos. Life on the streets was hard, but I got used to never knowing what to expect or where to stay.

As I got older, I got a job bartending, and one day a man with gold teeth came in to order a drink. He told me how beautiful I was, that I was in the wrong business, and how much more money I could be making if I came with him. He took me shopping and told me hundreds of men would pay to be with me. I felt confused - loving the attention but still afraid. He took pictures of me, posted them online, and before I knew what was happening, he was pimping me out. He wouldn't give me any money, and I eventually ran away from him.

I found myself alone, guilty, and disgusted. Who could I tell? I couldn't let anyone find out what I'd done.

I was now 17, and through an Internet search, I located my real dad. We were reunited for the first time since I was born, and he picked me up in his eighteen-wheeler. He treated me like an adult and started buying me alcohol; we were having a blast. Then, one night I woke up with him on top of me. I didn't know what to think, and we never talked about it. It wasn't long before he started pimping me out at truck stops.

I was miserable. I was called names like "little whore" daily, and he would belittle me and watch everything I did. I couldn't even go to the bathroom by myself; he'd stand outside waiting.

He used me for his own pleasure, groped me, and called me his property. I wanted out, and I complained and begged him to stop touching me. He got mad and left me behind in Seattle, Phoenix, Indianapolis, and Tennessee. Each time I would call him begging to come back and get me because I was afraid to ask the other strangers for help.

It was a vicious cycle, and I finally just gave up. I was so beat down and tired. I didn't care anymore. I thought of myself as a dirty, nasty whore with a drug problem. I thought nobody wanted me.

After a suicide attempt, I reached out for help, and a counselor called P.A.T.H. They told me that they wanted me and loved me just as I was. I was given Ms. Louise (Allison) as a mother figure, who won't ever give up on me or push me away. She doesn't call me names or scream at me even when I do things wrong. I always thought of myself as bad, unwanted, and a lost cause, but she showed me that was not true.

I was raised doing magic spells with my mom, and I believed in worshipping many different gods and goddesses. I couldn't understand this "one and only God" I kept hearing about at P.A.T.H., but I learned about Jesus by watching godly people very closely.

From the very start, Ms. Louise was so loving and forgiving that I understood her God's grace, and I chose to follow Jesus and got baptized. I really wanted what she had.

Now, my body is healthy, and my mind is restored. I'm filled with peace, and all I had to do was reach out and ask for help. I have gained so many treasures since I've been at P.A.T.H. including self-esteem and confidence. I can look people in the eye. I've gained sisterhood and family relationships that I never had before. I love that I can take a shower without a man watching me and sleep in a bed alone without waking up to some creep on top of me. I can trust people now.

I am loved and now I see what it is like to love others. I want to pass this love on by helping other broken women by saying, "Hey I know right where you are, I've been there" and "I know those feelings." There are no lost causes. I'm so glad I didn't give up and kill myself. I believe I'm here for a reason, and God has a special plan for me.

Understanding freedom is at the crux of addressing sex trafficking. It's not just physical freedom we want for victims. We want each person involved (victim, john, and trafficker) to experience a holistic freedom so they can live the very best life possible, and it would be disingenuous to talk about freedom for others if we're not embracing that freedom for ourselves. That's why we're spending this week looking at the different facets of the gift God has given us.

Let's continue by reading Galatians 5:1-5.
(YouVersion app or www.Bible.com)

The apostle Paul begins by saying, *"It is for freedom that Christ has set us free. Stand firm, then, and do not let yourselves be burdened again by a yoke of slavery." (v.1)* The very reason why Jesus came to this earth as God in the flesh and defeating sin and darkness on the cross was for you and I to have FREEDOM!

Freedom from sin and selfishness and a self-led life.

Paul warns them not be burdened again by something that would oppress or enslave us. He goes on to use the example of circumcision, because it was a current-day issue the Galatians were wrestling with. In that day, there were some Jewish Christians who believed that a number of the ceremonial practices of the Old Testament (i.e., circumcision) needed to be followed by Gentiles who were converting to Christianity and becoming followers of Jesus.

You can imagine the conversation with a 40-year-old Gentile convert..."If you don't get circumcised, you don't really love Jesus. You're not one of us!" That probably didn't go over too well.

Paul recognized this outward step of circumcision was just the beginning, and it would ultimately culminate in a Christian's need to take on the Law (all the rules and regulations of the Old Testament) which Christ set us free from. The result would be a tremendous burden on the Christian to do all the right things to pay God back or earn the freedom that was originally freely given.

How often do we do things to "earn" something from God?

If I just read my Bible every day,
go to church every weekend,
give money to the church,
go on a mission trip,
or help out with the latest "cause" that pops up...

We can't pay God back for what He's done for us nor can we "earn" something from Him. What we can do is participate in activities that position us to be transformed.

Helping those who are vulnerable and broken is not something we do because it will somehow make us look good in the eyes of God. It's not out of guilt or a need to make ourselves feel better.

Paul says, *"The only thing that counts is faith expressing itself through love."* (v.6)

Faith...expressing itself...through love.

We're not earning. We're not paying back. We're not bribing God for a blessing. We're just loving, because He loved us first. We're using our freedom to help those who are in need of hope.

💡 TIME TO REFLECT

1. **Do you ever feel the pressure to pay God back or do something in order to be a "good Christian"? Why or why not?**

2. What does it practically look like to "express your faith through love"?

PRAYER

"God, thank you for the gift of freedom and grace. Help me to embrace it without feeling the need to pay you back or earn it in some way. I want to use this freedom to make a difference in the world. I want everyone to experience true freedom in their lives."

QUOTE OF THE DAY

"I do not at all understand the mystery of grace - only that it meets us where we are but does not leave us where it found us."
Anne Lamott #inplainsightfilm

INSTAGRAM IT!

"I do not at all understand the mystery of grace - only that it meets us where we are but does not leave us where it found us."
Anne Lamott

InPlainSightFilm.com

Being Wise With Our Freedom

At the moment we choose to follow Jesus and turn our life over to him, God floods us with grace and mercy. All of our mess-ups, screw-ups, and foul-ups have been wiped clean – past, present, and future.

Nothing we do can diminish God's grace or love for us.
That's an amazing amount of freedom.
The question becomes…what do we do with this freedom?

Let's read 1 Corinthians 6:12-20.
(YouVersion app or www.Bible.com)

Paul says we can do anything we want…but it might not be beneficial.

Can I choose to drink, eat, say, think, or do anything with my body and know that God has already forgiven me? YES! But, is it benefiting me or the other people in my life? Maybe…maybe not.

Even though this question can apply to many things in our lives, Paul specifically focuses on our sexuality. If we are now part of the Body of Christ with the Holy Spirit living inside of us, how do we want to use our physical bodies? Is our behavior expressing love or selfishness?

Paul even goes so far to ask…how could you pay to have sex with some-one when you know how precious your sexuality (and your body) truly are?

How about objectifying the woman walking down the street…?
Watching porn on the Internet…?
Going to a strip club…?
Getting an erotic massage…?
Having sex with a prostitute…?

Is any of that honoring the sacred temple of the Holy Spirit...your body? Are you expressing a genuine love for the person who is participating in the experience with you?

Paul writes, *"You are not your own; you were bought at a price. Therefore honor God with your bodies" (v.19-20).* When we honor our bodies and honor the people around us, we're simultaneously honoring God.

We have been given this life-giving freedom for a reason. It's not so we can go on sinning with the knowledge that we'll be forgiven for whatever we do. We've been given this freedom to make a positive impact in this world.

We have freedom to...

→ Embrace the uniqueness of our personality –
   not needing to compare ourselves.
→ Leverage our strengths for the benefit of others –
   not needing to prove ourselves.
→ Serve those who are vulnerable and broken –
   not needing to congratulate ourselves.

How will you use your precious freedom today?

💡 TIME TO REFLECT

1. What are you doing on a regular basis that is not "beneficial" to yourself or others?

2. Is there something you could start doing instead that would be more beneficial?

3. What action steps can you take today to make that shift?

 **PRAYER**

"God, thank you for the incredible freedom to do anything with my life. Help me to understand the responsibility that comes with this gift, and help me use it wisely. I want to utilize my mind, body, and heart to make a positive difference in this world."

 **QUOTE OF THE DAY**

"A hero is someone who understands the responsibility that comes with his freedom."
Bob Dylan #inplainsightfilm

 **INSTAGRAM IT!**

"A hero is someone who understands the responsibility that comes with freedom."

Bob Dylan

InPlainSightFilm.com

DAY #13
Who Will You Set Free?

Over the last week, it's become crystal clear that we have an incredible gift of freedom, and we have the opportunity to use it to make a positive impact in the world.

Let's begin by reading Luke 4:14-21.
(YouVersion app or www.Bible.com)

As he stood up in the synagogue, Jesus reads a passage from Isaiah and says, "This is what I'm all about. This is what I'm here to do." If that's Jesus' mission, then why aren't we focused on the same mission 2,000 years later? Going to church, attending a small group, and donating money are all great...but it seems like Jesus had something else in mind.

As followers of Jesus, we have been chosen to...
share the good news of God's grace,
bring physical, emotional, and spiritual freedom to the oppressed,
open the eyes of people who can't see a vision for their lives,
set people free from those who would enslave them,
and proclaim to the world that God is good and loving.

How can we live this out? Not out of guilt. Not out of a need to pay Jesus back. Not to bribe God for a blessing. Not out of a need to prove ourselves. We live this out most powerfully when...

- **We love, because He first loved us.**
  As we become aware of how much God loves us in our own state of vulnerability and brokenness, we are motivated to be a funnel of His love and grace toward others.

- **We serve, because Jesus invites us to serve with him.**
  Jesus is still at work in this world doing all the same things through the power of the Holy Spirit and the hands of those who have chosen to follow him.

This kind of motivation is both long lasting and sustainable. The bottom line is that our world is filled with people who need freedom, and you and I have tasted it through the grace of God. If this "freedom" remains just a bunch of spiritual talk, most people will never even sample it.

People need to experience the freedom firsthand.

That's where you come in. Your city is full of people who are vulnerable and broken. What are you practically doing about it?

1. How would you compare what Jesus is all about (Luke 4:14-21) with what many churches and Christians are focused on?

2. If Jesus came to Earth to bring freedom, there must be a lot of people in need of it. As you think about your city, who are the groups of people in need of more physical, emotional, financial, relational, and spiritual freedom?

3. Turn to the back of the book and read through the "31 Ways to Take Action" again. Which one catches your attention most, and why?

PRAYER

"Jesus, I see that you came into this world to bring freedom. Help me to be more aware of the people in my city who are oppressed in some way. Open my eyes to their plight, and help me see how I can take action."

QUOTE OF THE DAY 🐦

"Nobody's free until everybody's free."
Fannie Lou Hamer #inplainsightfilm

INSTAGRAM IT! 📷

"Nobody's free until everybody's free."
Fannie Lou Hamer

InPlainSightFilm.com

GOD IS AT WORK

JEANNE ALLERT, Founder
The Samaritan Women - Baltimore, MD

When I was 18, I was thrust in front of a podium and had to give a college speech for a large audience. Instead of being terrified, as most people are to speak publicly, I was hooked. Over the next 25 years, I would travel the globe as a professional speaker, presenting on technologies and trends with the Internet. It was a glamorous lifestyle, and people paid a lot of money to have me pontificate on a topic (that I know now) had very little consequence.

What I didn't realize is that the majority of my professional life was just "God's Boot Camp" preparing me and honing a set of skills that would be used when He deemed ready. In 2007, God pulled me out of that industry, planted my feet on new ground, and opened my eyes to an issue of REAL consequence - human slavery. What could be of greater eternal consequence than the redemption of God's people? The impact of the message He's now asked me to carry is so overwhelming that I find I've traded my "puffed-up speaker confidence" for a posture of humble fear and awe. With a new posture, I now see everything quite differently.

God is at work in all of us, in every detail of our lives.

There is no "chance" to where we are, what we're doing, or who we're with. God is masterfully knitting together each experience and relationship for His purpose. Now, as I stand before audiences with a new message, I know God has a purpose for all this. I'm affirmed in that truth, because almost every time I speak, there's some young girl, parent, or pastor who comes up to me afterwards and shares how this heinous business has touched their lives.

As we serve these survivors of horrendous trauma and brokenness, I hold within me the absolute conviction that everything she's suffered has been under His watch, and He will use it for His glory. Coming to the realization of God's sovereignty doesn't just change how I see things...it changes EVERYTHING.

67

While it may be tempting to skip over the "Belong" and "Celebrate" sections because they stretch your group, you'll be missing out on a time of intimate connection and growth.

There's no need to rush. Let people share their learnings, but be sure everyone has a chance to speak (not just the most talkative people).

 **BELONG**

Take time to go around the group and answer this question...

"As you think back to your childhood, what is a profoundly positive memory that stands out in your mind?"

 CELEBRATE

Let's take some time quiet our hearts and focus our minds. Turn to the back of this book to sing along with these two hymns. Don't worry about what your voice sounds like. Just sing to God. Before singing, take a moment to pray and ask God to remind us of these timeless truths as we worship Him.

"Grace That Is Greater" – Building 429
"Come Thou Fount Of Every Blessing" – Mark Schultz

GROW

Every few weeks, we hear a news report of a missing child, or we see an Amber Alert on a flashing billboard. While it can cause us to pause momentarily, most of us continue on about our business, because we don't know the child or someone related to them.

There is a distance that prevents us from engaging and taking action. You may remember in the film when James Pond with Hope for Justice says, *"Once you know about this, you have to do something about it... instead of being overwhelmed and paralyzed by it, you need to take a step back and think about what would you do for your own daughter."*

What would you do if your son or daughter were involved in sex trafficking (or some other nefarious situation)?

In response to the accusation that he welcomes sinners and eats with them, Jesus tells three parables back-to-back with a powerful theme that can inform our posture toward those who find themselves "far from home."

Let's open our Bibles and begin by reading Luke 15:1-10.

1. When you lose something (a family pet, car key, your cellphone), how do you feel? What do you do?

2. In both parables, the person's reaction is the same. What did they want their friends and neighbors to do? Why?

3. Jesus connects this common life situation (finding something that was lost) and turns it into a spiritual lesson. How important is "finding" someone in the eyes of Heaven? Why?

Let's continue reading Luke 15:11-31.

4. As you think about people you have known who have run away from home, become addicted to a substance, or gotten caught up in crime, what do you think drives them (us) to "set off for a distant country" so to speak?

5. What do you think "home" represents in the story?

6. From the way Jesus tells the story, can you imagine the father looking, watching, and waiting for his son to come back home? From what happens, what do you think was going on in the father's heart while his son was far from home?

7. It is clear that our Heavenly Father welcomes those who are "lost" in some way. In fact, the apostle Paul writes, "For I am convinced that neither death nor life, neither angels nor demons, neither the present nor the future, nor any powers, neither height nor depth, nor anything else in all creation, will be able to separate us from the love of God that is in Christ Jesus our Lord." (Romans 8:38-39 – NIV)

How could this impact your life if you embraced Paul's words as being true?

8. In your own words, describe the older brother's attitude and actions.

9. Is your heart more like the older brother or the father when you think about "johns" (people who purchase sex)? How about when it comes to "pimps" (those who traffic children and women)? Why?

10. What would it practically look like to have God's heart for those who are "far from home" – those who are vulnerable and broken?

SERVE ⚙

Frankly, it's unrealistic to think that every one of us can help every hurting person that comes across our path. Andy Stanley, founder of North Point Ministries, is known for saying, *"Do for one what you wish you could do for everyone."*

Last week, you may have talked about some ways your group can take action together. **Is God nudging members of the group to say "yes" to any of the "31 Ways to Take Action" at the end of this book?**

Leader Note: Choose several people to pray for the items below, or break into smaller groups of 2-3 people.

→ Pray for the women and children in your community who are currently being sold for sex. Pray for their rescue and restoration.

→ Pray for your group to have wisdom on how to take action together.

→ Ask God to help you start "doing for one what you wish you could do for everyone."

In the midst of vulnerability and brokenness, despair can roll in like a thick fog over the landscape of life, and it prevents us from seeing the possibilities that lie in front of us. Without hope, there is little motivation to take action, because...

"Things just aren't gonna get any better."
"Nothing ever goes my way."
"Nobody cares about my situation."

Have you ever heard any of this hopeless negativity swirling around in your head? We all have from time to time, but people who are deeply struggling in life hear it more often than not. When you lose a sense of positive expectation about the future, you've lost hope.

Open your Bible and begin by reading Romans 5:1-5.
(YouVersion app or www.Bible.com)

Hope is "a strong and confident expectation." The reason why many of us lose hope in the midst of turmoil or suffering is because of *where* we are looking for it. If we're looking for clues solely based on our outward circumstances, life can seem pretty grim if things aren't going well for us. That's why it's important to ask, "Where does my hope come from?"

The apostle Paul says that *"we boast in the hope of the glory of God" (v.2)*, which means that our strong and confident expectation is based on God's presence and power in our lives.

If we draw our hope from God, then a positive expectation isn't tied to external circumstances. Hope can actually produce joy and peace in the midst of suffering, because we know that God has a good plan for our lives. We know that our present circumstances are producing perseverance, which ultimately develops character.

All of this is possible if, and only if, we trust in God as our Source.

In Romans 15:13, Paul writes, *"May the God of hope fill you with all joy and peace as you trust in him, so that you may overflow with hope by the power of the Holy Spirit." (NIV)*

That's what we're ultimately looking for, isn't it? Joy and peace. Paul points us toward the God of hope who ultimately supplies us with everything we're truly longing for. Let's look to Him to provide what only He can provide.

 **TIME TO REFLECT**

1. **Why is hope so important to us as human beings? What happens when we lose hope?**

2. **What would it be like to look to God as the source of your hope - instead of outward circumstances?**

3. **As you connect with people who have lost hope in an area of their lives, what encouragement can you give them?**

PRAYER 🛜

"God, you are the Source of my hope, and I am choosing to have a positive expectation toward the future. I trust you, and I believe you have a great plan for my life. Help me to share this hope with people in the midst of despair."

QUOTE OF THE DAY 🐦

"Hope is being able to see that there is light despite all of the darkness."
Bishop Desmond Tutu #inplainsightfilm

INSTAGRAM IT! 📷

Take a photo with your phone and post on Instagram!

From Guilt to Self-Forgiveness

Yesterday, we learned that hope emerges in our hearts as we put our trust in God who has a great plan for our lives - no matter what we may be experiencing in our present circumstances. As this positive expectation of the future develops, it can be obscured by feelings of guilt about what got us into our current situation.

Remember, we're not just talking about "those people" who are needy in our world...we're talking about you and me. We're coming to grips with the fact that we're all vulnerable and broken in some way, and we desperately need God's power and presence to bring hope and healing.

Guilt - the kind that's debilitating and condemning - gains a foothold in our hearts when we don't embrace God's incredible grace for ourselves and continually ruminate on whatever shortcomings we see in our past.

Think for a moment about all the things you think you "should" have done in order to live up to whatever expectation you had (or have) for yourself.

I should have chosen to _____.
I should have saved my _____.
I should have waited until _____.
I should have gone to _____.
I should have said _____.

Here's the deal - you didn't do whatever it was! It's over. It's done. You can't go back and change it. All you can do is make decisions today that align with your values and desires for the future.

If you're still kicking yourself over past decisions, NOW is the time to forgive yourself in the same way that God has *already* forgiven you. Holding yourself hostage to sins of the past or unrealistic expectations is only going to hold you back from living a great life right now.

Let's read Galatians 2:15-16 in The Message:

"We Jews know that we have no advantage of birth over "non-Jewish sinners." We know very well that we are not set right with God by rule-keeping but only through personal faith in Jesus Christ. How do we know? We tried it - and we had the best system of rules the world has ever seen! Convinced that no human being can please God by self-improvement, we believed in Jesus as the Messiah so that we might be set right before God by trusting in the Messiah, not by trying to be good."

The apostle Paul - a Jew - was writing to followers of Jesus to help them understand the grace found in God's forgiveness, which is available to us through the death and resurrection of His Son. He makes it clear that it's not about our personal efforts to live by the rules or do everything just the right way. Whose voice matters most? The Voice of God speaking grace and forgiveness over your life? Or, that voice of condemnation holding you to your past mistakes and decisions?

Forgive yourself in the same way that God has already forgiven you.

💡 TIME TO REFLECT

1. **Be honest with yourself. Make a list of things that you hate about your past - things you haven't forgiven yourself for.**

   -
   -
   -
   -
   -
   -
   -
   -
   -
   -
   -

2. What do you sense God is saying to you today about these things?

 **PRAYER**

"God, I present this list of things in my past to you, and I release each one of them based on your grace. I accept your forgiveness, and I'm choosing to forgive myself. Help me to feel that forgiveness and cleanse my mind from the painful or harmful memories. I'm trusting you with my future."

 **QUOTE OF THE DAY**

*"To forgive is to set a prisoner free and discover
that the prisoner was you."*
Louis B. Smedes #inplainsightfilm

 **INSTAGRAM IT!**

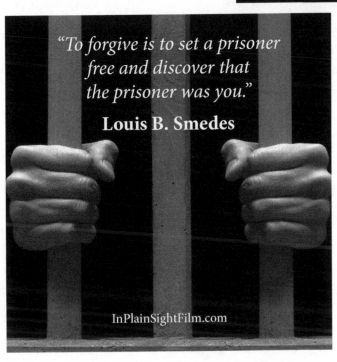

79

NEVER GAVE UP HOPE

Dennis & Barbara (parents of "Button" who is featured in the film)

We don't know what we can offer as parents of a daughter that has been trafficked, because we really don't understand it ourselves.

We are an upper middle class family living in an upper middle class suburb on the East Coast. We're an educated, intact, healthy family. Our daughter was adopted at three days old, and she was the center of our universe. She was loved and wanted for nothing. Starting in her teenage years, she became defiant, grades slipped, lying became the norm, and her new circle of friends left much to be desired. It seemed like normal adolescent rebellion, but it just kept getting worse. As her behavior began to spin out of control, we sent her to five different counselors, two psychiatrists, and a neurological doctor. Through all of this, she never had any interest in drugs or alcohol, but she was put on many different medications and diagnosed bipolar.

By 19, she was running away from home for weeks at a time.

We thought she would end up dead because of the crowd she was hanging with. In desperation, we took the suggestion of her psychiatrist and sent her far away to a rehab center for two years. Maybe, she was mentally ill.

Little did we know at the time, the process of grooming her for "the Life" had already taken hold. She had slipped out of our hands and into the hands of traffickers who corrupted all that she'd known and instead taught her "the Game." She was coerced to lie about her situation and tell us just what we needed to hear to continue our support. She would go missing for long periods of time, being sold across several states. She finally reappeared to us when we were contacted by a vice detective in Las Vegas. It was then we began to understand that our beloved daughter was not mentally ill, but enslaved in a world we couldn't understand and couldn't reach. At this point, we had to release her with love. We didn't know what else to do.

The vice detectives in Las Vegas were angels in uniforms; they truly care about the welfare of these girls, but the hold on these girls is stronger than any of us realize. In 2012, after she was brutally beaten by a pimp, the detectives put her in a safe house and offered her a chance to free herself from these heinous men. They contacted The Samaritan Women who secured a plane ticket for her and was ready to give her a new start in Baltimore.

Of course, still not thinking she was worthy of a better life, she ran away again, and we didn't hear from her for a year.

The violence, deception, abuse, and constant relocation continued. To this day we don't know all of it and don't want to. We'll never forget the night she called from a convenience store in Connecticut and finally asked for help. It was perhaps one of the hardest moments in this journey. We had to tell her that she could come home, but she couldn't stay. She had to get help for herself. She then contacted The Samaritan Women and asked for a second chance, and we were thankful to hear that The Samaritan Women had been praying for our daughter all along. We drove her to Baltimore, and let her go once again.

We never knew places like The Samaritan Women existed.

Over the past several months, we have watched the daughter we knew return. She wasn't bipolar. She doesn't need to be medicated or institutionalized. She needed to have the toxins from that world cleansed from her and to discover her own worth once again. Thankfully, she's getting all of that at The Samaritan Women. She's receiving counseling to deal with her fears, engage her emotions, and dig deep to figure out why she thought she was never worthy of happiness. She is taking college classes and is very involved with her church. She has become a leader in the home and is even becoming an advocate for those who are living what she lived. She's organized a street outreach, and she's testified at a state Senate hearings on human trafficking legislation. We are so proud of her.

We never gave up hope, and our prayers were answered.

DAY #17
From Anger to Healing

It is said that holding onto anger is like drinking poison and expecting the other person to die. I know it's truly painful. It wasn't right. There's no excuse...

> People intentionally hurt you.
> They said they would do one thing, and they did another.
> They said they'd always be there, and they left.
> They emotionally and/or physically assaulted you.
> They disappointed you.
> And...it hurts.

When you talk with anyone who is "stuck" in life, you'll eventually hear about the people who have hurt them and the angry poison they continue to drink - thinking it will make the painful memories of the offender go away. When we see other people allow anger to boil over time, we recognize how useless all that energy truly is. Yet, when we drink the poison ourselves, it's hard to see how much damage it's causing us.

Let's take a few moments to read Psalm 37.
(YouVersion app or www.Bible.com)

David writes, *"Refrain from anger and turn from wrath; do not fret—it leads only to evil. For those who are evil will be destroyed, but those who hope in the Lord will inherit the land." (v. 8-9)*

He's not suggesting that we ignore the evil or deny that the pain isn't real, but there's a deep trust in God's ultimate plan. Over and over in this psalm, the theme of turning from anger and trusting in God shines through.

Retaliation - an eye for an eye - is so common in our lawsuit-filled culture. Yes, in some cases, justice must be served, but my guess is that you're not looking to sue that friend who never returned the book they borrowed from you. You're not going after the family member who let you down or the co-worker who isn't pulling their own weight.

Feeding the anger only causes you pain. Healing is available as we extend forgiveness (just as we've been forgiven) and trust God as we delight in Him. Embrace this reminder from David...*"The Lord makes firm the steps of the one who delights in him; though he may stumble, he will not fall, for the Lord upholds him with his hand." (v. 23-24)*

TIME TO REFLECT

1. **When you think back over the course of your life, who are you still angry with? Who do you resent?**

2. **When we hold on to the anger or resentment, we often receive a conterfeit payoff or "false benefit" that we may enjoy. As you think about the resentments above, what false benefit are you receiving?**

   ❑ Feeling like they owe me something.
   ❑ Believing I'm a better person than they are.
   ❑ Receiving sympathy from people around me.
   ❑ Holding that person hostage because of what they did.
   ❑ _____

3. **Can you imagine what you would feel like if you were to forgive them, release the resentment, and experience freedom from that experience in the past? What's holding you back?**

PRAYER 📶

"God, I need your help to release this anger and resentment. In the same way that you have forgiven me, I want to forgive _____.
I release the resentment now, and I invite you to heal my heart. Thank you for giving me freedom from the poison I've been drinking."

QUOTE OF THE DAY 🐦

"Anger is an acid that can do more harm to the vessel in which it is stored than to anything on which it is poured."
Mark Twain #inplainsightfilm

INSTAGRAM IT! 📷

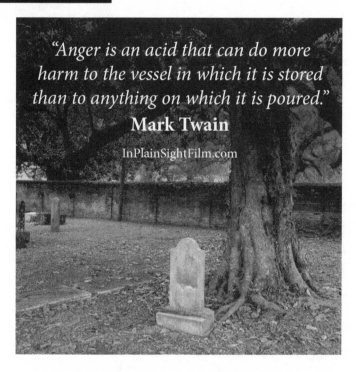

"Anger is an acid that can do more harm to the vessel in which it is stored than to anything on which it is poured."
Mark Twain

InPlainSightFilm.com

From Indifference to Love

Holocaust survivor, author, and Nobel Peace Prize winner, Elie Wiesel writes, "The opposite of love is not hate, it's indifference. The opposite of art is not ugliness, it's indifference. The opposite of faith is not heresy, it's indifference. And the opposite of life is not death, it's indifference."

It's easy to find ourselves in a state of indifference, isn't it?

We've been hurt by others.
We're busy with our own lives.
We're overwhelmed by the needs around the world.
And, we don't want to be taken advantage of.

Sound about right?

Yet, is that *really* the way we want to live? Don't we want to live in such a way that we generate more hope in the people around us? Don't we want to do more than just *talk* about making a difference in this world?

You've probably heard or read the apostle Paul's description of love in 1 Corinthians 13 many times, but don't allow it's familiarity to prevent you from experiencing it in a fresh way today.

Read 1 Corinthians 13:1-8 and soak it in.
(YouVersion app or www.Bible.com)

Love is not an emotion - something that we fall in and out of. Yes, feelings can be associated with it, but love is a choice. It's an action verb. It's something we do. If we want to make this world a better place, it starts with love - not just a nebulous desire to be a do-gooder - but a choice to do practical things that benefit other people.

Guess what? If we start making the choice to do what is loving, the feelings associated with love will soon follow. Love first, feel later.

1. **What happens in our world when people are indifferent to the plight of the vulnerable and broken?**

2. **Re-write Paul's description of love in your own words by filling in the blanks below. Then, read the new description as one complete statement.**

Love is _____ (patient),

love is _____ (kind).

It does not _____ (envy),

it does not _____ (boast),

It is not _____ (proud),

It does not _____ (dishonor others),

it is not _____ (self-seeking),

it is not _____ (easily angered),

It keeps _____ (no record of wrongs),

Love does not _____ (delight in evil)

but _____ (rejoices with the truth).

It always _____ (protects),

always _____ (trusts),

always _____ (hopes),

always _____ (perseveres).

Love never _____ (fails).

3. In light of your own definition of love on the previous page, would you be willing to ask yourself this question throughout the day?

"What would be the loving thing to do or say right now?"

 **PRAYER**

"Holy Spirit, open my eyes to the ways I am indifferent to the people and situations around me. Help me recognize what the loving thing to do or say would be, and nudge me to take action in that moment. I don't want to stand by and do nothing. I want to be a source of love in this world. "

 **QUOTE OF THE DAY**

"The opposite of love is not hate, it's indifference."
Elie Wiesel #inplainsightfilm

 **INSTAGRAM IT!**

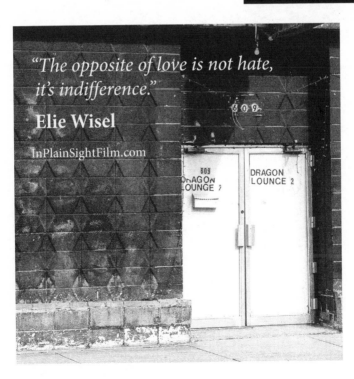

 **DAY #19**

From Loneliness to Community

Without a community of people to share the ups and downs of life with, seasons of vulnerability and brokeness can settle in to become a way of life rather than a short period through which we learn and grow. We're not talking about familiar faces you see at church every weekend or those high school friends who you just 'friended' online. We're talking about a community of people who know what's going on in your life...people who have your back and are cheering you on.

Let's take a few moments to read 1 Corinthians 12:12-27.
(YouVersion app or www.Bible.com)

Essentially, Paul is saying, "Every single person is needed in the Body of Christ", but I'm wondering if there's not a broader truth being shared that applies to the entire world. Not only does every person have inherit value, but we each have a special role to play on this planet.

For some of us, we don't think we have much to offer...
* I don't have any special talents.
* I lack the experience needed to contribute.
* I really don't have the time or money to help.

Other of us have a different challenge...
* I don't want to work with those people.
* I just need to focus on my own family.
* I can do it on my own without any help.

Whether you tend to be lacking confidence or feeling overly self-sufficient, the truth is that we all need each other. Specifically, we need a group of people who know us by name, who know when we're struggling, and who we can walk alongside when life gets tough for them as well.

Your community isn't just a place you live...it's the fabric of people interwoven through your life.

Notice how Paul describes how a body works and likens it for our need for one another, *"The eye cannot say to the hand, "I don't need you!" And the head cannot say to the feet, "I don't need you!" On the contrary, those parts of the body that seem to be weaker are indispensable, and the parts that we think are less honorable we treat with special honor."* (v. 21-23)

I am needed.
You are needed.
We need each other.

Without intentional action steps, this type of community rarely forms on its own. Someone has to go first...to walk across the room, send the first message, make the first call, and extend an invitation.

Remember what it's like to feel wanted. Ignore the fear of rejection for 30 seconds, and reach out to someone today. You'll be glad you did.

 **TIME TO REFLECT**

1. List 2-4 people you speak with on a weekly basis who truly know you and what's going on in your life.

2. If you were to describe the type of community (close, supportive relationships) you want for others (and yourself), what would it look like?

3. Who are 2-4 people you would like to develop this type of community with?

4. What action steps do you sense you need to take in order to nurture those types of relationships in your life?

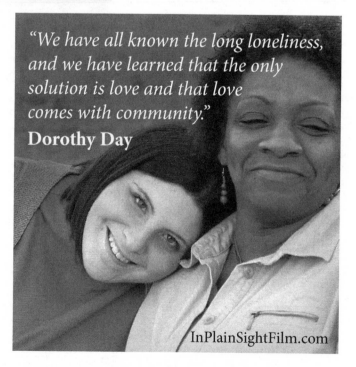

"We have all known the long loneliness, and we have learned that the only solution is love and that love comes with community."
Dorothy Day

InPlainSightFilm.com

From Brokenness to Restoration

Throughout this week, we've been looking at shifts available to each one of us through the power and presence of Jesus in our lives. Although immediate, supernatural change is possible, much of the transformation we experience is gradual and most clearly seen when we look back over the course of a difficult season of life.

It can be tempting to allow painful experiences (whether caused by others or brought on by our own choices) to linger and become the "new normal" for our lives.

- Broken relationships.
- The loss of a loved one.
- Addictions or unhealthy habits.
- Results of bad decisions (financial, relational, physical).
- Emotional, spiritual, or physical abuse (received or given).

Although we live in a broken world where these things are part of everyday life, these negative experiences don't have to define our lives. We don't have to live under the weight of the things that have been put on us (or we've put on ourselves).

Let's read Romans 8:1-4 in The Message...

"With the arrival of Jesus, the Messiah, that fateful dilemma is resolved. Those who enter into Christ's being-here-for-us no longer have to live under a continuous, low-lying black cloud. A new power is in operation. The Spirit of life in Christ, like a strong wind, has magnificently cleared the air, freeing you from a fated lifetime of brutal tyranny at the hands of sin and death.

God went for the jugular when he sent his own Son. He didn't deal with the problem as something remote and unimportant. In his Son, Jesus, he personally took on the human condition, entered the disordered mess of struggling humanity in order to set it right once and for all. The law code, weakened as it always was by fractured human nature, could never have done that.

The law always ended up being used as a Band-Aid on sin instead of a deep healing of it. And now what the law code asked for but we couldn't deliver is accomplished as we, instead of redoubling our own efforts, simply embrace what the Spirit is doing in us."

Although our sins have been forgiven and this "deep healing" is intantaneous in the eyes of God the moment we turn our lives over to the leadership of Jesus, we spend our days "embracing what the Spirit is doing in us." The Holy Spirit - the same power that raised Jesus from the dead is living within you, and you have the opportunity to cooperate with what the Spirit is doing.

Instead of saying, "I can't get beyond this...",
start saying, "God is transforming me from the inside out."

Instead of saying, "I'll never be able to...",
start saying, "The Holy Spirit is giving me the power I need."

Feel the difference?

Although our full restoration back to who God created us to be won't come to fruition until the day we come face to face with Him, the Bible is telling us that we have access to healing and transformation during this in between time.

The Holy Spirit is already at work, and our part is to start embracing what the Spirit is doing in us. No one has to live under a "continuous, low-lying black cloud" any more!

💡 TIME TO REFLECT

1. **In what area of your life do you long for restoration, transformation, or healing? Why?**

2. What would it practically look like to start embracing what the Spirit is doing within you like Paul encourages in Romans 8:4?

 **PRAYER**

"Holy Spirit, I trust that you are already at work within me. I invite you to soften my heart, heal my mind, and give me the courage to release whatever I need to let go of. Bring life to those parts of me that are dead, and restore me to who God made me to be."

 **QUOTE OF THE DAY**

"The best way to cooperate with God's healing work in your soul is to go find other people who are hurting and be a blessing to them."
Joyce Meyer #inplainsightfilm

 **INSTAGRAM IT!**

A NEW SUPPORT SYSTEM

Michelle (mother of a 12 year old victim)

When my daughter was 12 years old, she moved from my home in southern California to her father's house up north, and that's where she met her cousin's wife who was 19. Initially, it started out as a new familial relationship, but it soon turned into what I now know is called "grooming".

This 19 year old family member would have my daughter and my niece together a lot - talking to them about boys and relating to them on a teenage level. It soon turned into, "Let's go out to AM/PM tonight to get a snack," but they'd end up at an apartment complex where they would be meeting strangers. She would teach them how to meet people online in chat rooms, and it would go from fun and playful to very explicit.

This was all happening when she was spending the night with her cousin at my sister's house with her father's permission.

I started getting calls from her school saying that she was sick. Her mouth and eyes would swell, and I'd never seen anything like that. I finally said, "You need to come home to southern California." When she came home, I recognized that she had gone from being a little girl who participated in things and got good grades to getting straight Fs and skipping school.

Six months after she moved back to my home, she finally came out with her story. I thought, "Oh my God, what does this mean?" At that moment, my heart just sunk. Come to find out...she had been taught how to have phone sex, how to interact on websites, and how to post profiles. She said that most of the incidents were on the phone or computer, but there were three incidents with physical contact "where it wasn't sex because they didn't want to get me pregnant." My daughter said that she had not wanted to say anything, because she didn't want the burden of breaking up her cousin's marriage to his 19 year old wife. On top of that, she just thought these were her "boyfriends".

I didn't know who to call, so I called my employee assistance program, and they stayed on the phone with me all night long. They called Child Protective Services, and they made a plan with me to contact her pediatrician and make a police report. Before that night at the police station, I had never heard the term "sex trafficking". It was very overwhelming, and I didn't know how to process it all. I didn't know who to be mad at. These were strangers who had hurt my daughter, and the only person to track down was a 19 year old girl who was now divorced and out of the family picture for other reasons unrelated to the situation with my daughter. The night they were scheduled to do a forensic interview to go through all that had happened to her...she ended up in a psychiatric hospital, because she had tried to kill herself. She couldn't physically handle all of this. That changed my entire goal...from pursuing justice to making sure she was safe and going to fully heal. My focus was now on getting her treatment.

When I found out about Courage Worldwide, I sent them an email and gave them a brief synopsis of what had happened. Within five minutes of talking with them, I saw my daughter completely relax, because they understood what she had gone through. They were so loving and reassured me that I was doing the right thing. Over the course of the year she was at Courage, I would go up to visit her monthly. Initially, she was very defiant and resistant, but they helped her understand that she needed to *want* to be there. We worked a lot on the communication dynamics that would prepare her to live in a normal environment again after having been exposed to such extremes. The team of people at Courage were amazing, and they became an extension of her family.

Prior to her coming back home, we made sure she had a new support system in place, and she was able to re-integrate back into everything she initially had. In fact, she just got her first job, and her grades are getting back to where they used to be. The reality is...even after she moved home, there have been challenges, because these issues don't just go away. Even though Courage House isn't part of her daily life, she still calls them, and they even support me through challenging moments.

I don't know where my daughter would be without Courage Worldwide.

This week, we make a distinct shift from inner work toward a life of action and service. Some group members will have a difficult time seeing how they can make a positive difference in the world, and you have the opportunity to help them see that God *can* and *will* use any willing servant. Our world needs every single person to do their unique part.

 **BELONG**

Take time to go around the group and answer this question...

"As you think back on your life, when was a time when God used you to make a positive difference in the world?"

 CELEBRATE

Let's take some time quiet our hearts and focus our minds. Turn to the back of this book to sing along with these two hymns. Don't worry about what your voice sounds like. Just sing to God. Before singing, take a moment to pray and ask God to remind us of these timeless truths as we worship Him.

"Rock of Ages" – Page CXVI
"Great Is Thy Faithfulness" – Elijah Young

📄 **GROW**

One of the most amazing things about this life is that God invites us into the process of restoration. Not only does God restore our own lives, but He calls us to be part of the process of restoring others and even the world at large.

Wouldn't it be ludicrous to follow Jesus (i.e., be a Christian) and NOT participate in God's plan of restoration? It would be like receiving a lavish gift and choosing not to share it with anyone. The truth is that we get the privilege of being "ministers of reconciliation" to help bring healing to this world, and our lives are transformed in the process.

➜ We start to see life from the perspective of others.

➜ We become less consumed with our own challenges.

➜ We realize how blessed we are.

➜ We increase our level of thankfulness.

➜ We are drawn back to what's truly important.

Jesus models it for us, and now the Holy Spirit empowers us from within. God has chosen you and me to be His messengers of hope in this world. Can you believe that?

Today, we'll be reading the words of the apostle Paul as he addresses followers of Jesus in the city of Corinth. This passage captures a moment in time in Paul's life, but the truths echo some 2,000 years later.

Let's begin by reading 2 Corinthians 4:5-12 in The Message:

"Remember, our Message is not about ourselves; we're proclaiming Jesus Christ, the Master. All we are is messengers, errand runners from Jesus for you. It started when God said, "Light up the darkness!" and our lives filled up with light as we saw and understood God in the face of Christ, all bright and beautiful.

If you only look at us, you might well miss the brightness. We carry this precious Message around in the unadorned clay pots of our ordinary lives. That's to prevent anyone from confusing God's incomparable power with us. As it is, there's not much chance of that. You know for yourselves that we're not much to look at.

We've been surrounded and battered by troubles, but we're not demoralized; we're not sure what to do, but we know that God knows what to do; we've been spiritually terrorized, but God hasn't left our side; we've been thrown down, but we haven't broken.

What they did to Jesus, they do to us—trial and torture, mockery and murder; what Jesus did among them, he does in us—he lives! Our lives are at constant risk for Jesus' sake, which makes Jesus' life all the more evident in us. While we're going through the worst, you're getting in on the best!"

1. As you read this passage, how do you think Paul sees himself? How would he answer the question, "Who are you?"

2. Paul writes, *"We carry this precious Message around in the unadorned clay pots of our ordinary lives. That's to prevent anyone from confusing God's incomparable power with us."* What stands out to you in this statement?

3. What is this "precious Message" that Paul refers to? Is it more than a verbal salvation message? What is it all about?

4. Are you aware of "God's incomparable power" within you (an unadorned clay pot)? Why or why not?

5. Paul seems to see the "troubles" of life through the lens of God's incomparable power. What would happen in your life if you started to see personal troubles and the world's troubles through that lens?

Let's continue with 2 Corinthians 4:13-18 in The Message:

"We're not keeping this quiet, not on your life. Just like the psalmist who wrote, "I believed it, so I said it," we say what we believe. And what we believe is that the One who raised up the Master Jesus will just as certainly raise us up with you, alive. Every detail works to your advantage and to God's glory: more and more grace, more and more people, more and more praise!

So we're not giving up. How could we! Even though on the outside it often looks like things are falling apart on us, on the inside, where God is making new life, not a day goes by without his unfolding grace. These hard times are small potatoes compared to the coming good times, the lavish celebration prepared for us. There's far more here than meets the eye. The things we see now are here today, gone tomorrow. But the things we can't see now will last forever."

6. How would your life (and the lives of people around you) be different if you believed that "every detail works to your advantage and God's glory"?

7. So many things can cause us to give up on doing good in the world and focus on the safety and satisfaction of our family. What tends to hold you back the most?

  ❑ Feelings of inadequacy   ❑ Busyness
  ❑ Fear of the unknown   ❑ Selfish with my time
  ❑ Fear of failure or criticism ❑ Want to hold on to my money
  ❑ Assuming God will use   ❑ Uncomfortable to deal with
     someone else   "those people"

  ❑ _____

  ❑ _____

  ❑ _____

8. What's at stake in our world if we're unwilling to partner with God in the process of restoring the vulnerable and broken?

9. What would happen if you truly embraced the fact that God wants to use you to make a positive difference in the world?

10. What's holding you back from embracing that fact today?

SERVE

My guess is the Holy Spirit is nudging your heart to take action on behalf of the vulnerable and broken. Usually, it only takes about 30 seconds of courage to get started. You know what you need to do. You've been thinking about it for a couple of weeks. Fill in one or more blanks, and share with the group what you're committed to doing this week.

→ I will make a call to _____.
→ I will sign up to _____.
→ I will make a donation to _____.
→ I will volunteer to _____.
→ I will _____.

PRAYER

Leader Note: Help people partner up (one on one) to pray together.

→ Ask the person you're praying with, "What's holding you back from taking action? How can I pray for you?"

(👫) DAY #22
A Heart of Compassion

As we've been embracing God's heart for the vulnerable and broken over the last three weeks, we've been learning that...

- God loves you...and "those people."
- God wants freedom for all...starting with you.
- God has the power to heal and restore.

Yet, at some point, we need to take tangible action steps if we're going to follow Jesus in his mission of setting the oppressed free. Did you know that according to current estimates there are 27 million slaves in our world today - more than any other time in our world's existence? In describing sex trafficking in the United States, Amanda Rodriguez, Prosecutor in Baltimore County, Maryland, states, *"Young women and young men that are caught in this are actually victims. They're being manipulated and coerced, and they're slaves."*

Our nation is in need of abolitionists to take on this challenge, and that's why we're turning our attention to six characteristics we all want to cultivate in our lives as followers of Jesus. Are you ready to become an abolitionist?

Let's begin by reading Matthew 9:35-38.
(YouVersion app or www.Bible.com)

An abolitionist is one who is committed to doing his or her part to abolish slavery in this world. It doesn't mean you need to start rescuing victims or tracking down traffickers tomorrow, but cultivating compassion is a great start.

Notice Jesus' response as he travelled from village to village and recognized that *"they were harassed and helpless, like sheep without a shepherd."* His heart was moved, and he had compassion on them. Jesus didn't say, "Well, they really should have planned ahead for the future" or "If they just worked a little harder, they could get ahead." He recognized their vulnerability, and he knew that workers were (and are) needed to help. When you hear about (or see) someone in a challenging situation, what's your first response? Indifference or compassion...or somewhere in between? Without compassion, our efforts toward service will fade when the people we're serving don't respond as we'd wish.

What happens when we invest time, energy, and money in someone or something, and the growth we hoped for doesn't develop? Do we give up and find someone to blame? Or, do we remind ourselves that people are vulnerable, broken, and in need of compassion? Do we go back to why we are passionate about this issue to begin with? The truth is that people are enslaved around the world...including in the United States, and no one deserves to be treated like property. No one. When your compassion starts to wane, put yourself in that person's shoes by asking a few questions...

→ What would I experience on a daily basis?
→ Would I have the freedom to do whatever I want?
→ What would it be like for someone to verbally, physically, and sexually assault me daily?

Compassion isn't something we're just born with.
We can actually cultivate it.

 **TIME TO REFLECT**

1. Do you consider yourself an abolitionist? Why or why not?

2. Why is compassion so important in the fight against slavery?

3. As you think about our world, how are people "harrassed and helpless, like sheep without a shepherd"?

PRAYER 📶

"Jesus, I want to see people through your eyes. Help me to let any indifference in my heart fade away, and replace it with compassion for those who are challenged in this world. Help me feel what you feel."

QUOTE OF THE DAY 🐦

"As Christians, our compassion is simply a response to the love that God has already shown us." **Steven Curtis Chapman #inplainsightfilm**

INSTAGRAM IT! 📷

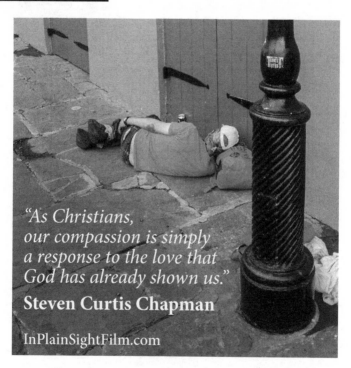

"As Christians, our compassion is simply a response to the love that God has already shown us." **Steven Curtis Chapman**

InPlainSightFilm.com

Take a photo with your phone and post on Instagram!

While "social justice" can evoke politically-charged persuasions one direction or another, the Bible is clear about God's heart for the "least of these" (Matthew 25:31-46). Listen for the call to action that can't be ignored by followers of Jesus...

Deuteronomy 10:17-18 says, *"For the Lord your God is God of gods and Lord of lords, the great God, mighty and awesome, who shows no partiality and accepts no bribes. He defends the cause of the fatherless and the widow, and loves the foreigner residing among you, giving them food and clothing." (NIV)*

Proverbs 31:8-9 says, *"Speak up for those who cannot speak for themselves, for the rights of all who are destitute. Speak up and judge fairly; defend the rights of the poor and needy." (NIV)*

James 1:27 says, *"Religion that God our Father accepts as pure and faultless is this: to look after orphans and widows in their distress and to keep oneself from being polluted by the world." (NIV)*

Time and again, the Bible calls attention to the orphan, the widow, and the foreigner – people who were not able to fend for themselves or had no support system. The nation of Israel was commanded by God to care for the vulnerable and broken, and their eventual failure to do so was part of the reason they were judged and sent out from the land.

As followers of Jesus, we are called to be instruments of God's justice in this world. At the heart of the word, "justice" means to treat people equitably, and this plays out in two primary ways in the Scriptures...

• Punishing wrongdoers no matter their race, education level, position, or socio-economic status.
• Righting the wrong that has been done by caring for victims and those with the least economic and social power.

Doing one without the other will only leave a gap in our society. Those who do wrong must be held accountable, and those who lack power must be unshackled.

If the Bible speaks of God's concern about orphans, widows, and foreigners, you better believe that He's just as concerned about the plight of the poor, the elderly, single parents, foster children, those with HIV/AIDS, those who lack homes, people moving from other countries, and victims of sex trafficking.

Yes, there are many different opinions on how to practically help these groups of people, but one thing is clear. God is passionate about bringing justice to each one of them, and radical generosity is one of the marks of living justly.

The key to developing a passion for justice is to understand that this isn't something just for a particular political party, denomination, or group of people. This is God's heart, and we're simply coming into alignment with what God is concerned about.

💡 TIME TO REFLECT

1. **As you think about your own community, who are the current day orphans, widows, and foreigners, and how do they lack power?**

2. **Re-read Proverbs 31:8-9. As a modern-day abolitionist, what would it look like for you to speak up for those who can't speak?**

3. As you think specifically about sex trafficking, what wrongs need to be righted? What justice needs to be provided to the trafficker, the john, the victim, and our communities as a whole?

 **PRAYER**

"God, help me to bring my heart into alignment with your passion for justice. Guide me away from earthly vengeance and toward Your desire for righting the wrongs that have been done to people in our world."

 **QUOTE OF THE DAY**

"Injustice anywhere is a threat to justice everywhere."
Martin Luther King, Jr. #inplainsightfilm

 **INSTAGRAM IT!**

"Injustice anywhere is a threat to justice everywhere."

Martin Luther King, Jr.

InPlainSightFilm.com

REDEEMED BY GRACE

EMMA, Survivor of Sex Traficking
Redeemed - Houston, TX

After having my daughter at 18 and breaking up with my boyfriend a few years later, I moved back into my Mom's house and worked as a pharmacy tech for over six years. In my search for love, I was partying, hooking up a lot, and ultimately fell for the wrong guy. I thought he really loved me, but within six months, he got me started working - doing something good "for us" as he called it.

I took my daughter to her father and asked him to keep her for a couple months, because that's how long my boyfriend (trafficker) said we would need. Well, I should have never believed that lie. My trafficking lasted six and a half years - jumping from motel to motel, state to state, and city to city.

Every time he hit me, yelled at me, or choked me out, I found a way to make it my fault.

By the time we made it to Texas, I hated working, and I started to really hate myself to the point that I stopped looking in the mirror as I got ready everyday. Not only did I lose custody of my daughter, but I lost my pharmacy license and even my driver's license. Most of my family and friends were gone - house, cars, and worst of all - I lost my soul. I didn't feel like a woman anymore, and I lost all respect for myself.

I got to the point where I was just surviving each day.

One Friday night, I called my cousin in a panic, because I knew things were about to get even worse. I told her what hotel I was staying at, and she made a lot of calls to help me out. That night, people from the YMCA picked me up and put me in another hotel. Two days later, I made a called to Redeemed, and that was the best decision I've made in the past seven years.

Over the past 12 months living at Redeemed, it has been one of the hardest and most freeing years of my life.

I say it's been hard, because I'm trying to regain my identity, starting to look in the mirror, and ultimately discovering who I am in God. Most difficult of all, I'm forgiving my trafficker for everything he did to me, and that's a big step in finding my freedom. Now that I've graduated from the Redeemed program, I'm discovering that it's still not easy having freedom in the real world.

I have God on my side, and I have the most amazing people backing me up.

I still can't go back to my home town, because it isn't safe for me, but I wouldn't want to be anywhere else at this moment of my life. I miss my family a lot - especially my daughter - but I know she's in good hands with her father and step-mother. And, at least I can talk to her on a regular basis. I'm now headed to a six-month, Christian discipleship program, and I'm trusting that everything I've been through will be used for God's glory.

I'm trusting that He's going to make sure nothing I've been through will ever go to waste.

DAY #24
A Hunger for Wisdom

Have you ever known someone who watched one documentary or read a single book and then thinks they're an expert? Don't get me wrong. Passion is needed for us to abolish slavery in our world, but humble wisdom is an attribute that all of us should seek to cultivate.

Why? Because there will always be someone who knows more or has more experience on a subject than you do, and a posture of learning and growth allows us to work together to end this heinous crime against humanity.

Let's hear from Solomon in Proverbs 4:1-9 in The Message.

"Listen, friends, to some fatherly advice; sit up and take notice so you'll know how to live. I'm giving you good counsel; don't let it go in one ear and out the other. When I was a boy at my father's knee, the pride and joy of my mother, He would sit me down and drill me: "Take this to heart. Do what I tell you - live! Sell everything and buy Wisdom! Forage for Understanding! Don't forget one word! Don't deviate an inch! Never walk away from Wisdom - she guards your life; love her - she keeps her eye on you. Above all and before all, do this: Get Wisdom! Write this at the top of your list: Get Understanding! Throw your arms around her - believe me, you won't regret it; never let her go - she'll make your life glorious. She'll garland your life with grace, she'll festoon your days with beauty."

Our learning can't just focus on facts, figures, and book knowledge; it's about developing an understanding of a subject so that it ultimately matures into wisdom.

Wisdom is personified in the words of Solomon. She guards your life, keep an eye out for you, and she makes your life glorious. How? By preventing you and me from making immature decisions and avoidable mistakes.

If God wants to use us to be His messengers of hope and healing in this world, we need to develop...

> **Knowledge** - information about a subject.
> **Experience** - practical observations & real-life encounters.
> **+ Good Judgment** - the ability to apply knowledge & experience.
> **WISDOM**

Wisdom isn't something that develops overnight. It's an attribute that we're constantly developing as we gain more knowledge, experience, and good judgment. It's something that's more caught than taught, and we would be smart to start (or continue) hanging around people who are older or more experienced than we are.

TIME TO REFLECT

1. **As you look back on your life, when was a time when you wish you would have had more wisdom? What was missing from the formula above?**

2. **Why is humble wisdom important if we're going to work with others toward abolishing slavery?**

3. **Think about a wise person in your life you admire. Describe what makes them so wise.**

PRAYER 🛜

"God, help me to humbly learn from others who have walked before me. Give me the courage to ask questions, seek knowledge, and lean in to new experiences. With each opportunity I have to make a decision, may I slow down to listen to Your voice and seek Your guidance."

QUOTE OF THE DAY 🐦

"If I am through learning, I am through."
John Wooden #inplainsightfilm

INSTAGRAM IT! 📷

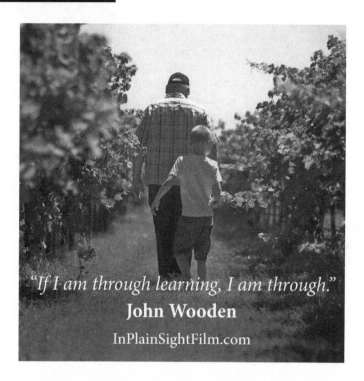

"If I am through learning, I am through."
John Wooden
InPlainSightFilm.com

A Willingness to Collaborate

When an issue like sex trafficking catches your attention, it can be tempting to dream about starting your own initiatives (especially if you're the entrepreneurial type). On the other extreme, you may feel overwhelmed and paralyzed - not knowing where to even begin.

Listen to Solomon in Ecclesiastes 4:9-12 in The Message...

"It's better to have a partner than go it alone.
Share the work, share the wealth.
And if one falls down, the other helps,
But if there's no one to help, tough!

Two in a bed warm each other.
Alone, you shiver all night.
By yourself you're unprotected.

With a friend you can face the worst.
Can you round up a third?
A three-stranded rope isn't easily snapped."

There's no possible way we can abolish slavery (or any other significant issue) without working together. There's not a single person (or organization) that has all the resources needed in order to combat the heinous crimes being committed against women and children in our nation. The bottom line is that we need each other.

As you think back to the documentary, you may recall the words of Stacia Freeman, US Director of Hope for Justice, as she said, *"If we don't link arms, engage, and start sharing what I know and what you know and start sharing information, I don't know if we'll ever address this issue in our lifetime. If our goal long-term is to eradicate sex trafficking, it's going to require partnerships."*

There are some incredible benefits to collaborating with others...

→ You get the benefit of another's strengths.
→ They can minimize your weaknesses or shortcomings.
→ You gain a fresh perspective from the experiences of another.
→ There's no need to carry the weight alone.
→ You increase your support network.
→ Any risk can be lessened.

We're not just referring to starting an organization with someone. We're talking about having an attitude that welcomes the support of others and looks for ways to work together with a spirit of collaboration.

When it comes to making a positive difference in this world, the words of Solomon could not be more true, *"It's better to have a partner than go it alone. Share the work, share the wealth. And if one falls down, the other helps, but if there's no one to help, tough!"*

💡 TIME TO REFLECT

1. **What are some reasons why someone would not be open to collaborating with others?**

2. **Think back to a time when you collaborated with someone on a project? What were the benefits?**

3. **What strengths do you bring to any working relationship you develop?**

"God, give me an open heart to connect with others who are passionate about bringing hope and healing to our world. Protect my mind from being territorial or closed off to the ideas of others. I am open to divine appointments and trust you to bring people and organizations into my life who I can work alongside."

 **QUOTE OF THE DAY**

"If our goal long-term is to eradicate sex trafficking, it's going to require partnerships."
Stacia Freeman #inplainsightfilm

 **INSTAGRAM IT!**

"If our goal long-term is to eradicate sex trafficking, it's going to require partnerships."
Stacia Freeman

InPlainSightFilm.com

 **DAY #26**
A Readiness to Take Action

Merely talking about an issue can raise awareness (which is good), but nothing is going to be accomplished until someone is courageous enough to take action. This isn't about what type of personality you have or how much time or money you have at your disposal. Taking action is a spiritual issue.

Listen to the words of Jesus' brother in James 2:14-19.
(YouVersion app or www.Bible.com)

James begins by asking, *"What good is it, my brothers and sisters, if someone claims to have faith but has no deeds?"* We can feel warm and fuzzy about God's love and the fact that we're forgiven for our sins, but what about the mission of Jesus?

While preaching about the Kingdom of God, Jesus demonstrated life in the Kingdom. He was modeling the way of life that he wanted his followers (you and me) to live through the power of the Holy Spirit (who was sent after Jesus ascended to heaven).

This way of life includes...

→ Sharing a message of His forgiveness which produces hope.
→ Using our words to bless rather than curse.
→ Healing relationships through forgiveness.
→ Demonstrating love to our enemies.
→ Investing our resources to help those in need.
→ Setting people free from whatever enslaves them.

The truth is that taking action is messy. It's easier to remain comfortable in a state of inaction and just worry about our own concerns. Yet, that posture is antithetical to life in the Kingdom. Jesus (along with his brother James) calls us to a way of life that is concerned about the vulnerable and the broken.

Believing in God and His grace is wonderful, but that's not what it means to be a follower of Jesus. To follow Jesus means that we are actually becoming more and more like him...willing to take action on behalf of others...trusting him with the results.

Believing in him is good, but taking action based on our beliefs is what he is calling us to.

💡 TIME TO REFLECT

1. **Think about someone you know who demonstrates both "faith and deeds." What is attractive about their life?**

2. **Why is taking action on behalf of others messy?**

3. **As you think about sex trafficking in the United States, what is the cost of us not taking action?**

PRAYER

"God, I want to be ready to take action. Help me overcome any fears or laziness that holds me back, and give me the courage to take that first step. I am choosing to follow in the footsteps of Jesus and take action on behalf of the vulnerable and broken in my community."

QUOTE OF THE DAY 🐦

"There are risks and costs to action. But they are far less than the long range risks of comfortable inaction."
John F. Kennedy #inplainsightfilm

INSTAGRAM IT! 📷

"There are risks and costs to action. But they are far less than the long range risks of comfortable inaction."
John F. Kennedy
InPlainSightFilm.com

A Commitment to Persevere

One of the greatest attributes in the life of an abolitionist is perseverance - to remain committed to the cause despite difficulty or delay in achieving success.

Let's read Hebrews 12:1-3 in The Message...

"Do you see what this means - all these pioneers who blazed the way, all these veterans cheering us on? It means we'd better get on with it. Strip down, start running - and never quit! No extra spiritual fat, no parasitic sins. Keep your eyes on Jesus, who both began and finished this race we're in. Study how he did it. Because he never lost sight of where he was headed - that exhilarating finish in and with God - he could put up with anything along the way: Cross, shame, whatever. And now he's there, in the place of honor, right alongside God. When you find yourselves flagging in your faith, go over that story again, item by item, that long litany of hostility he plowed through. That will shoot adrenaline into your souls!"

This passage gives us profound instructions on how to persevere in the face of opposition, delay, or disappointment...

1. Be inspired by those who have gone before us.
2. Rid ourselves of anything that would hold us back.
3. Keep our eyes on Jesus as our primary example.
4. Study how Jesus stayed focused on his Father's mission.
5. Recognize that full restoration and our ultimate reward is eternal.

We live in a culture where perseverance and faithfulness is rare. We bounce from job to job and relationship to relationship when things become difficult. Because there are so many options in our world, we know that we can simply move on to something else if we're even slightly frustrated or discouraged. There are some incredible benefits to working through challenges that arise.

119

Although there are times to change course if something is not showing signs of fruit, we would be wise to hang in there and push through whatever is holding us back from experiencing our desired results. What would happen if we were willing to...?

> → Look for creative ways to overcome obstacles.
> → Work through relational difficulties.
> → Release any personal need for something to be just one way.
> → Discern what we can learn in the process.
> → Reach out for wisdom from those who have gone before us.
> → Trust Jesus with the results.

Can you imagine the results? Not only would we have more personal peace in our lives, but I bet we can push through most of those obstacles as we collaborate with one another. Let's commit to persevere together.

💡 TIME TO REFLECT

1. **Think about a time in your life when you persevered through something difficult. What enabled you to make it through?**

2. **As you think about making a difference in the lives of the vulnerable and broken, what do you need to persevere through right now?**

3. **If you're willing to work together with people in your community and persevere through challenges, what do you think could be possible?**

"Jesus, you are my primary example of how to persevere in life. I have allowed obstacles to hold me back from bringing hope and healing into my community, and I need your help to push through. Give me the courage to follow your lead and trust you with the results."

 **QUOTE OF THE DAY**

"If you are going through hell, keep going."
Winston Churchill #inplainsightfilm

 **INSTAGRAM IT!**

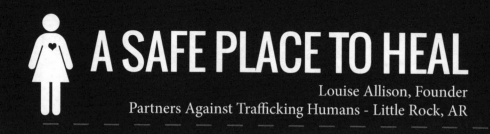
I was raised in a loving home, but my step-dad started approaching me in an uncomfortable sort of way when I was 12 years old - not coming on strong, but as a friend. I later found out that he was "grooming" me for something more. On my 14th birthday, he took advantage of me sexually, and I left the house vowing never to return.

Only two blocks from my house in the Highland Park area of Dallas, Texas, I was picked up by a really nice man who, after a lengthy conversation, offered to get me to a safe place for the night. That started the two-year nightmare of being sold on the streets.

I shut down emotionally and went through each day robotically - going where I was told to go and doing what I was told to do.

The only emotion I had was an intense desire for death. I tried a number of times to kill myself through overdoses, but kept waking up, vowing to do a better job next time. I was arrested several times, but I was trained to give an alias and lie about my age...so I did.

I was arrested for the last time at the age of 16, and after two years in boarding school, I graduated with honors. Yet, on the inside, I was still a beaten, raped little girl filled with shame and fear, so I did the only thing I knew to do. I returned to the streets.

Now, as an 18 year old prostitute, my pimp decided he didn't want me with other men, so he married me and kept me isolated without phone or transportation. I was completely submissive to all types of abuse and felt as if I deserved it. We had children together, and after 14 years of marriage, I began coming out of the fog, filed for divorce, and later went for help in a "life recovery" center.

I found women who loved me, not in spite of what I'd done, but because of who I was.

I developed a relationship with a loving God and began to heal from over 20 years of hiding beneath the cloak of fear, shame, guilt, self-condemnation, depression, and suicidal thoughts. The suicide monster finally left me, and the depression soon followed. I began to experience peace and real happiness for the first time since I was very young. I thank God for places that minister to victims of sexual assault and love us when we don't feel lovable.

I now have the privilege of working with others who have been victimized through sexual exploitation.

It is both a blessing and an honor to be able to love women and children who feel unlovable. As strange as it may sound, I'm grateful that I can "sit in the pain" with them and say that I know what it's like to be beaten, raped, and to have things done to us that we don't even know about because of the drugs. It is somehow comforting when we know we're not alone.

I thank God for healing me and allowing me to have a safe place for others to heal.

It's one thing to talk about doing good in the world, but it's another thing to actually take action. As a leader, you have the opportunity to model this in your own life and invite group members along on the journey.

What are you doing to take action, and how are you inviting them to participate with you?

 **BELONG**

Take time to go around the group sharing something that impacted you from the last six days of devotional reading. Be sure to share your name if you've just started meeting or if there's someone relatively new in the group.

What inspired or challenged you?

 **CELEBRATE**

Let's take some time quiet our hearts and focus our minds. Turn to the back of this book to sing along with these two hymns. Don't worry about what your voice sounds like. Just sing to God. Before singing, take a moment to pray and ask God to remind us of these timeless truths as we worship Him.

"Nothing But the Blood" - All Sons & Daughters
"All Hail The Power Of Jesus' Name" - Point Of Grace

 GROW

If you've read any of the Bible or even listened to a handful of sermons, you've probably heard some pretty amazing stories about men and women who have been called by God to do extraordinary things. In the New Testament alone...

→ John the Baptist preaches repentance and lives in the desert.
→ James and John leave their boat (and father) to follow Jesus.
→ Simon Peter and Levi left everything and followed him.
→ Stephen preaches against religious leaders and is stoned to death.
→ Paul travels extensively to preach and experiences great hardships.

Perhaps you've read one of the many Christian books on the market that hold these radical experiences up as an example of what it means to be a true Christian - to leave everything behind and follow an extra-ordinary call on your life. While God *does* call some of us to make radical decisions to leave things or people behind, most of us grow up, go to school, get a job, have a family, and live relatively 'normal' lives.

Think about it. What about all the followers of Jesus in the Bible that *didn't* travel around and preach to crowds of people? What about the people who owned businesses or worked for other people or were raising children? In the midst of daily life, weren't they able to love their communities right where they lived?

We believe that *all followers of Jesus* are called to bring hope and healing to their communities, and the way in which we live that out is unique and different for each one of us.

The question is, "What is God calling *you* to do?"

Let's read 1 Peter 4:1-11 in The Message:

"Since Jesus went through everything you're going through and more, learn to think like him. Think of your sufferings as a weaning from that old sinful habit of always expecting to get your own way. Then you'll be able to live out your days free to pursue what God wants instead of being tyrannized by what you want.

You've already put in your time in that God-ignorant way of life, partying night after night, a drunken and profligate life. Now it's time to be done with it for good. Of course, your old friends don't understand why you don't join in with the old gang anymore. But you don't have to give an account to them. They're the ones who will be called on the carpet - and before God himself.

Listen to the Message. It was preached to those believers who are now dead, and yet even though they died (just as all people must), they will still get in on the life that God has given in Jesus.

Everything in the world is about to be wrapped up, so take nothing for granted. Stay wide-awake in prayer. Most of all, love each other as if your life depended on it. Love makes up for practically anything. Be quick to give a meal to the hungry, a bed to the homeless - cheerfully. Be generous with the different things God gave you, passing them around so all get in on it: if words, let it be God's words; if help, let it be God's hearty help. That way, God's bright presence will be evident in everything through Jesus, and he'll get all the credit as the One mighty in everything - encores to the end of time. Oh, yes!"

1. In verses 1-4, what major shifts does Peter suggest in the life of a Jesus follower?

2. What does it practically mean to be "free to pursue what God wants instead of being tyrannized by what you want"? What would that look like for you?

3. In the paragraph above, Peter writes, *"Most of all, love each other as if your life depended on it."* Do you believe that our lives depend on loving each other? Why or why not?

4. God has given you talents, resources, and experiences to use as an abolitionist and God's messenger of hope and healing to the vulnerable and broken in your community. Notice the way that The Message and NIV state 1 Peter 4:10...

"Be generous with the different things God gave you, passing them around so all get in on it." (MSG)

"Each of you should use whatever gift you have received to serve others, as faithful stewards of God's grace in its various forms." (NIV)

What talents / skills do you have? What comes naturally to you?

❑ _____

❑ _____

❑ _____

❑ _____

❑ _____

What resources do you have to use? A home, computer, car, boat, camera, pool, money, time?

❑ _____

❑ _____

❑ _____

❑ _____

❑ _____

What experiences are part of your life story? Walking through a painful season of life, overcoming an addiction, organizing events, raising money, leading teams?

❑ _____

❑ _____

❑ _____

❑ _____

❑ _____

5. In the documentary, Jenny Williamson (founder of Courage Worldwide) challenges us by saying, *"Do what you love to do... for these kids. If you are a businessperson, help me figure out how to get sustainable funding for this so we can plan and we can build. If you're a musician, write a song for these kids. If you're an artist, paint a picture. If you're a filmmaker, make a film. Do what you love to do...for these kids."*

The idea is that you already have the talents, resources, and experiences needed to take action. Just do what you love to do. Take a minute and think about how you're uniquely positioned to take action in your community. What do you sense God is calling you to do?

SERVE ⚙

As your group wraps up the IN PLAIN SIGHT study, turn once again to the back of the book to read the "31 Ways to Take Action". Take time to read through them one by one around the group. After you're done reading each opportunity, discuss the question...

As a group, how can we begin to help abolish sex trafficking (i.e., a form of slavery) in the United States? What is our next step?

PRAYER

Leader Note: Help people partner up (one on one) to pray together.

➔ Ask the person you're praying with, "How is God calling you to take action, and how can I pray for you?"

 **DAY #29**
Guard and Guide Your Heart.

While compassion for the vulnerable and broken is something to be cultivated in the heart of every follower of Jesus, each one of us is captured by specific challenges in our world.

Not everyone will make sex trafficking *their cause*. We get that. Maybe God has stirred your heart for clean drinking water, orphans, environmental issues, or fair wages. At the same time, we also believe that all of us should be aware of sex trafficking in our communities and do *something* about it.

Let's read Proverbs 4:18-27.
(YouVersion app or www.Bible.com)

Not only are you walking on a path *"like the morning sun, shining ever brighter"*, but Jesus says that you are actually the *"light of the world!"* As one of God's messengers in this world, you have the capacity to be incredibly influential, and Solomon is warning you to guard your heart. Why? Because *"everything you do flows from it."*

In the ancient Hebrew culture, the "heart" represented a person's total being - their intellectual thought, emotion, memory, and desires.

Whatever captures your heart will ultimately be revealed in your life.

> → You'll think about it.
> → You'll talk about it.
> → You'll invest time and money in it.

Think back to your childhood. What were you really in to? Legos, Barbie, bikes, skateboards, computers, or fashion? You thought about it, talked about it, and invested time and money into it. It's no different now that you're an adult. What's in your heart...determines the path of your life.

Here's the great thing. Solomon makes it clear that we have an active role in what is allowed to capture our hearts. He says to "guard" it, which means that we can choose what we expose our heart to.

In fact, you've been exposing your heart to some powerful things just by walking through this devotional and group study guide. Great job! That's one way to direct your heart and open it up to new information and possibilities. Your heart is powerful, and you have the opportunity to give careful thought as to how it will guide your next steps.

💡 TIME TO REFLECT

1. **What tends to occupy your heart (and mind) most of the time during your average week?**

2. **While family and job responsibilites are the primary focus for most of us, how can you intentionally cultivate a heart awareness of important issues during your week?**

   ❑ Reading a book on a social justice issue.
   ❑ Searching for news articles about pertinent current events.
   ❑ Discussing what you've learned with a few friends.
   ❑ Inviting a local 'expert' out to coffee to ask questions.
   ❑ Praying for the vulnerable and broken in your community.
   ❑ _____.

3. **One of the ways to know what "cause" has captured your heart is to ask...**

   What makes you cry?
   What makes you angry?
   What keeps you up at night?
   What makes your adrenaline start pumping?

PRAYER

"God, thank you for giving me the ability to guard and guide my heart. I have seen and heard things that cause passion to rise up from within, and I don't want that fire to be snuffed out. Help me to cultivate those things within my heart and to take action in practical ways."

QUOTE OF THE DAY

"Are you bored with life? Then throw yourself into some work you believe in with all your heart, live for it, die for it, and you will find happiness that you had thought could never be yours."
Dale Carnegie #inplainsightfilm

INSTAGRAM IT!

"Are you bored with life? Then throw yourself into some work you believe in with all your heart, live for it, die for it, and you will find happiness that you had thought could never be yours." **Dale Carnegie** InPlainSightFilm.com

Take a photo with your phone and post on Instagram!

Find People to Work With.

Last week, we talked about how collaboration was one of the key attributes of an abolitionist, and now is the time to put that belief into action.

If you want to take the mission of Jesus seriously...
If you want to bring hope and healing to your community...
If you want to minister to the vulnerable and broken...
If you want to help stop sex trafficking in your area...
You must find people to partner with!

Let's see how Jesus sent out his disciples in Mark 6:6-13.
(YouVersion app or www.Bible.com)

Notice that Jesus sent them out in pairs and gave them authority to cast out evil spirits, preach the Good News, and heal the sick. Check out the long list of supplies Jesus told them to pick up on their way...a staff and sandals. I'm sure they were wearing clothes as well, but the point is that He wanted them to trust God to provide for their needs along the way.

When we hear about an issue as daunting as sex trafficking, it can be tempting to think that we need a huge team of people and a ton of money. What if you took a different approach?

→ What if you find at least one other person who is passionate about the issue?

→ What if you both start to pray for God's guidance?

→ What if you research what was already going on in your city, county, or state to combat the issue?

→ What if you reach out to a reputable organization to see how you can help what they're already doing?

→ What if you start to do what you love to do?

There are many well-meaning organizations that are sprouting up across our nation to fight sex trafficking, and we encourage you to research their mission, approach, and reputation. Here are some questions that are important to ask or research:

- Is the organization's mission and strategy clear to you?

- Are the leaders professionally equipped to carry out that mission?

- Is the organization simply focused on general awareness, or is it actually serving victims, working to decrease demand, or seeking to enforce justice?

- What is the reputation of the organization in the community?

- If it is an aftercare home, we would encourage you to look through the questions in the back of the book under "Who To Support."

♀ TIME TO REFLECT

1. As you think about people in your life, who would you like to partner with in order to take action together?

2. What are the talents, resources, and experiences that this person brings to the table?

3. Are there any organizations in your area (or in the nation) that you're already aware of? If not, are you willing to start researching this week to learn more?

"Holy Spirit, give me the courage to reach out to other people so that we can work together. This issue is too big for me to tackle alone, and I need the support and encouragement of others. I am trusting that You are already at work in their hearts as well."

 QUOTE OF THE DAY

"Alone we can do so little; together we can do so much."
Helen Keller #inplainsightfilm

 INSTAGRAM IT!

"Alone we can do so little; together we can do so much."
Helen Keller
InPlainSightFilm.com

DAY #31
Do What You Love to Do.

When it comes to making a positive difference in the world, it's funny how easily we dismiss what we love to do as not being "good enough" or somehow inapplicable to the cause. It's as if serving is supposed to be difficult, grueling, or painful in order for it to "count".

If God didn't want us to use what we love (our passions), why would He have even given us those desires or gifts to begin with?

Yes, there are those infrequent times when one of us *loves* to do something we're not really that good at, but for the most part, we love to do what we're gifted to do. In Group Session #5, we wrote down some talents, resources, and experiences that could be helpful as we look to take action. My guess is that what you love to do is embedded in that list.

Let's continue by reading Galatians 6:7-10 in The Message...

"Don't be misled: No one makes a fool of God. What a person plants, he will harvest. The person who plants selfishness, ignoring the needs of others - ignoring God! - harvests a crop of weeds. All he'll have to show for his life is weeds! But the one who plants in response to God, letting God's Spirit do the growth work in him, harvests a crop of real life, eternal life.

So let's not allow ourselves to get fatigued doing good. At the right time we will harvest a good crop if we don't give up, or quit. Right now, therefore, every time we get the chance, let us work for the benefit of all, starting with the people closest to us in the community of faith."

By discovering what we're passionate about, we'll be able to leverage what we love for the benefit of others. Notice that it's not about planting seeds of selfishness for our own glory, but it's about planting acts of service as a response to what God has given each one of us - unique gifts and talents.

The apostle Paul reminds us not to become fatigued or grow weary in the midst of doing good. If we're doing something we don't enjoy or we're not gifted to do, we'll burn out all the more quickly. That's why doing something we love to do is a great place to start.

What can we look forward to? Those seeds of service will sprout up into a good crop if we don't give up along the way.

 **TIME TO REFLECT**

1. **What activities or tasks give you the greatest feelings of satisfaction and pleasure? (Researching, planning, organizing, speaking, teaching, cooking, crafting, photographing, etc.)**

2. **How can you "do what you love" to bring hope and healing to your community and specifically to help stop sex trafficking?**

3. **What steps can you take this week to get started?**

   ❑ Call a friend to brainstorm about ideas.
   ❑ Reach out to a local (or national) organization to volunteer.
   ❑ Meet with a community leader to see how you can help.
   ❑ Connect with your pastor to discuss possibilities.
   ❑ _____.

PRAYER

"God, thank you for the way you have uniquely wired me. I am one of a kind! Help me to use what I love to do for the sake of others, and give me the motivation to get started right away. I realize what is at stake in my community, and I want to do my part."

QUOTE OF THE DAY

"If you can't figure out your purpose, find our your passion.
For your passion will lead you right into your purpose."
T.D. Jakes #inplainsightfilm

INSTAGRAM IT!

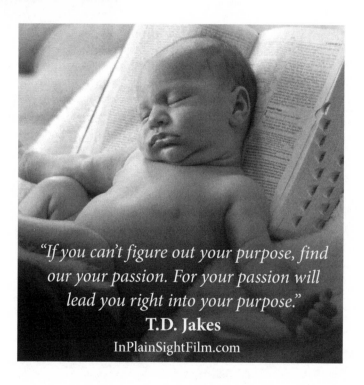

"If you can't figure out your purpose, find our your passion. For your passion will lead you right into your purpose."
T.D. Jakes
InPlainSightFilm.com

Raised in a small country town, I was a happy, outgoing, and bubbly child despite the darkness that surrounded me. I adored nature and all its beauty, and I could play for hours in the woods behind my house - pretending to fly away on a rope swing attached to a tree. I dreamed of becoming a famous singer or a veterinarian when I grew up.

While some kids worry about a monster under their bed, I was scared of the monster in my mama's head.

The first time she sold me was a couple weeks before my seventh birthday. At first, it was at seedy motels and her apartment, and then she started taking me to the homes of different men. Some of them took pictures and videos of me, and I felt so ashamed, dirty, and disgusting. Not only did she sell me, but she played twisted games and gave out horrific punishments - all of which seemed to be fueled by her addiction to drugs and alcohol.

When I got old enough, I finally ran away and ventured out to Hollywood on a Greyhound bus to try and make it as a musician. I soon found myself on the streets, and I literally sang for my supper.

Oftentimes, the same man would come to hear me sing and request "Amazing Grace" every time. I would sing the song, and he would talk to me about charity, God, and street kids like me. He seemed like he genuinely cared, and one day he made me an offer I couldn't refuse - to introduce me to a music producer. We met the next day as planned, and I got in the car (a choice I still cringe over). We drove a little outside Hollywood and chatted about music, where I was from, and his children. The next part is a bit hazy, but from what I remember, he stuck me with a needle, and I woke up to the smell of hay and animals. My eyes could hardly open, and I was gagged and chained to a barn stall.

As he raped me, he told me that I now belonged to him and the people he worked for. "If you try to run, I will kill you. If you do not obey me and do exactly as I tell you, I will kill you."

For the next 22 months, I was beaten, raped, sodomized, and worse. I never left that animal stall (chained and drugged everyday) unless it was to "work" for them - usually private parties on fancy boats, at high class hotels, secret clubs, private residences, or auctions.

What they didn't realize was that I had faced this type of evil before.

I held on to hope because I had escaped "hell" once before, and now I was going to get out again if it was the last thing I did. So, I started to plan my escape. As we left for our next scheduled trip, I hid the sleeping pills they regularly fed me, but I was still injected with heroin. When we stopped at a truck stop, he ordered food at the counter, and I told him I had to use the bathroom.

I stared at that bathroom window for a little while - thinking about what I would do once I got out. I pulled myself out the window, and I spotted a truck across the parking lot where a man was pumping gas. I took a breath, looked around, and ran as fast as I could to the truck. I opened the door, crawled in, and hid under the bunk in the truck's cabin.

I was trembling with fear, and I prayed that the driver wouldn't see me. "What if my owner catches me? Where was I going? What was I going to do?" I didn't care. What could he do that he hadn't already done...kill me?

I was finally free.

140

It's been 25 years since I escaped out that window, and I wish there would have been an organization to help me back then. It took some time to detox off the heroin they injected in me daily. I was haunted by my past, I partied, and I was in many abusive relationships. I had nightmares, anxiety attacks, flashbacks and blackouts. After many years of soul searching, I finally made a decision to start trying to heal my past - finding outlets for my pain and anger through music and art, but never going to any type of therapy.

Life was looking good, but there was still something off - still having black outs and losing time.

One day, I came across the Hope for Justice Facebook page, and I sent a message - sharing my story in hopes that it would help me heal even more and help others, too. I received a beautiful reply from Stacia Freeman that touched my heart, and I wept. We talked a bit here and there, and I felt compelled to tell her everything. I trusted her immensely even though we had never met.

Little did I know that by telling my story to her, my life would be changed.

She offered me the opportunity of a lifetime - to pay for my therapy, and she even found a qualified therapist in my area. I had come so far on my own, but I truly needed this. Therapy has been my saving grace. It has helped me more than I ever thought possible. I feel like a butterfly that's just hatched from its cocoon - ready to live a beautiful life!

I'm now 42 years old, and I live on a small, country farm, and it's truly my sanctuary. I am married to the love of my life, and we have two children who are happy and healthy. I call them my miracles, since I was told I would never have children because of the scarring inside. I now stand on a strong foundation and feel I am able to help others by sharing my story. I do not look at my life as a tragedy, but as an inspiration.

I want my story to touch people's hearts and give them hope that anything is possible.

For many people, childhood memories include things like ice cream, sunny days at the park, jumping jacks, and being spoiled by grandparents. For me, that was far from reality.

The first time I experienced shame was at the age of five when I was sexually and physically abused by my grandfather. That shame, along with anger, fear, and strong distrust of others, defined me for the next 40 years.

I carried the weight of those feelings, and it led me to a life of damaging thoughts and behaviors.

Several years ago I married a man only to have the dream of a family and white picket fence turn into a life of drugs, alcohol, and sexual assault. I was being sold by my husband to support our habit, and he would sweet-talk me into doing it "this one last time" as he drove me there and waited. After it was over, he'd call me names and sometimes hit me. This went on for 7 years.

My body became empty, dirty, and disease filled, and I felt nasty and worthless. Many people have asked, "Well, why didn't you just leave?" It's the same reason I didn't run away when I was a little girl.

I was held captive by my shame.

The feelings of anger and fear that began at the age of five had grown to the point that I didn't know life could be any different. My trafficker basically treated me how I expected to be treated.

Because of what had become of my life, I believed I didn't have a real purpose, and I wanted to die. I overdosed 17 times.

142

After the last overdose in October 2013, I signed myself into a rehab center, and they called P.A.T.H. After moving into the home, I began to heal - and mostly - I started an incredible spiritual journey.

Up until this point, I wasn't even sure there was a God.

I struggled so much with managing day-to-day life that I couldn't imagine a relationship with a God who could really love me, especially as nasty as I felt.

In November 2013, I accepted Christ as my Savior and was baptized three weeks later, which made it the best Christmas of my life. With my new relationship with God and the support of people at P.A.T.H., I am continually filled with the love and support I need to continue my recovery.

As a 46 year old woman, I thought my life was over, but it's only just beginning as God is replacing the shame, anger, and fear with the love, trust, and honesty I have always longed for.

Today, I stand not as a victim, but as an overcomer.

I have a strong, deep desire to make a difference in the lives of other hurting women. I didn't think there was hope for someone like me, but God has shown me differently.

May God bless you the way I've been blessed.

SEX TRAFFICKING 101 • How Could This Be Happening?

Note: This illustration depicts the most common process and associated reasons why sex trafficking unfolds in the United States. Yet, there are many ways in which this travesty occurs - involving both sexes in all three roles.

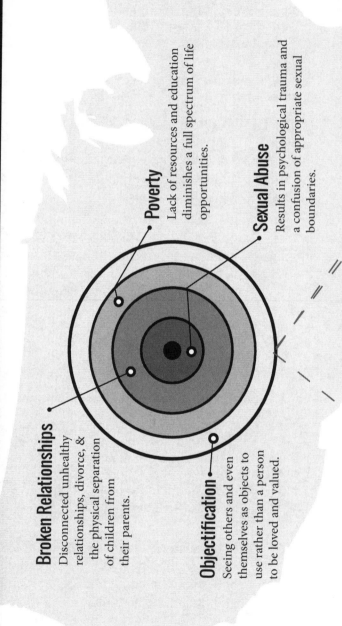

Poverty
Lack of resources and education diminishes a full spectrum of life opportunities.

Sexual Abuse
Results in psychological trauma and a confusion of appropriate sexual boundaries.

Broken Relationships
Disconnected unhealthy relationships, divorce, & the physical separation of children from their parents.

Objectification
Seeing others and even themselves as objects to use rather than a person to be loved and valued.

PORNOGRAPHY

XXX XXX XXX XXX XXX XXX XXX XXX XXX XXX XXX XXX XXX XXX

Widespread access and addiction fuels objectification of women and ultimately a desire to pay for an experience.

Victim

Customer / John

Sex Trafficker / Pimp

→ Women Are Here for Me to Use.
Perhaps, their father victimized women, or more than likely, they don't even know their father. They weren't taught what it means to be a loving man.

→ I Want to Be in Control.
With so many things feeling out of control, many men become manipulative and controlling in order to overcome feeling so out of control.

→ I Can Sell a Woman for Money.
To acquire money, support a drug habit, and/or buy possessions, a man comes to the conclusion that a woman can be sold for sex.

→ She is Vulnerable.
Through attention, gifts, and compliments, a man will profess "false love" with elaborate promises of a better life, fast money, and future luxuries.

STRATEGY

Recruiting - Targets vulnerable females, and professes false love.

Grooming - Breaks her down emotionally through manipulation and coercion, sexually through gang rape, and physically through violence.

Total Control - Keeps all or most money from her work at strip clubs, escort services, street walking, truck stops, massage parlors, hotels, or brothels.

Customer / John

→ **Women Are Here to Fulfill My Desires.**
Advertisements, movies, and music have told young men that a woman is an object to be lusted after or used for personal gain.

→ **I Deserve Whatever I Want.**
Between divorce, absent fathers, and domestic violence, many young men have no clue how to honor women or develop a healthy, intimate relationship.

→ **Pornography Fuels My Desires.**
With a desire to increase the feelings associated with viewing of explicit images, many men seek out a real-life experience to replicate what they've seen.

BUYING PROCESS

Shopping - Shops for a woman or child through websites where the victim is advertised or by driving to a local location such as known streets or truck stops.

Police Check - Asks to touch her (or vice versa) prior to arranging a transaction in order to ensure she is not an undercover officer.

Payment for Services - Has no regard for actual age no matter if she was advertised as "barely legal."

Victim

→ **I Was Sexually Abused as a Child.**
90% of prostituted women have been physically abused as children (Encyclopedia of
Women and Gender). When boundaries are
crossed, innocence is stolen, and there is a
confusion about what is normal, appropriate,
and healthy.

→ **I Am Often a Runaway.**
1 in 3 runaways is approached by sex trafficker within 48 hours of hitting the streets.

→ **I Am Vulnerable.**
In need of love, attention, or even shelter,
food, and clothing, she is vulnerable to the
offers coming from a trafficker.

→ **I Feel Stuck and Can't Leave.**
With a "chain around her brain", she can't
break away due to confinement, humiliation,
shame, dependency, and hopelessness.

NOT JUST AN INTERNATIONAL ISSUE

83% of victims in confirmed sex-trafficking incidents were identified as U.S. citizens.
(U.S. Department of Justice 2011 report)

Sex trafficking is modern-day slavery and involves the use of force, fraud,
or coercion to obtain a commercial sex act. It is the second largest
illegal crime in the world, right behind drugs.

SPOTTING THE SIGNS

Although a each victim of sex trafficking has a unique story, there are often some common, identifiable indicators. Victims will rarely self identify due to fear and coercion. By being aware of the signs, you may be able to save someone's life.

BLATANT SIGNS

→ Under 18 and is providing commercial sex acts.
→ In the sex industry and has a pimp, madam, daddy, family, or folks.
→ Forced, intimidated, or coerced into providing sexual services.
→ Believing their lives or family members' lives are at risk.
→ High security measures exist in their work and/or living locations (such as opaque windows, boarded up windows, bars on windows, barbed wire, security cameras, etc.)
→ Fearful of police and authorities.

POOR MENTAL & PHYSICAL HEALTH

→ Lacks health and dental care.
→ Appears malnourished.
→ Shows signs of physical and/or sexual abuse, physical restraint, confinement, or torture.
→ Fearful, anxious, depressed, submissive, tense, or nervous/paranoid.

LACK OF CONTROL

→ Not free to leave or come and go as she wishes.
→ Not in control of her own money, no financial records, or bank account.
→ Unpaid or paid very little.
→ Seem to be in debt to someone.

→ Has no identification or someone else is holding it.
→ Regularly moves to avoid detection.
→ Controlled by others through the use of drugs.
→ Not allowed or able to speak for themselves (a third party may insist on being present and/or translating).

UNUSUAL BEHAVIOR

→ Avoids eye contact.
→ Loss of sense of time.
→ Has few or no personal possessions.
→ Limited amount of clothing and a large proportion is sexual.
→ Motels or hotels are used as residential housing.
→ Fearful of telling others about their life situation.
→ Lack of knowledge of whereabouts and/or does not know what city she is in.
→ Claims to be just visiting and unable to say where she is staying.
→ Has numerous inconsistencies in her story.

INTERACTING WITH SOMEONE WHO MAY BE A VICTIM

Because sex traffickers brainwash their victims by repeatedly telling her that no one will listen if she tries to get help from the police or anyone else, many victims will be extremely closed off to encounters with others. That is why it is important to...

• Build trust through one-on-one interactions.
• Reassure her you are there to help - not to get them arrested.
• Avoid technical terms (sex trafficking) and be aware of "street terms" (the life, the game, my daddy, my folks).
• Be aware of canned stories such as "I'm just visiting," "I'm from out of town," or "I do this on my own because I want to."
• Do not be offended if she lies, and be sure not to take it personally.
• Avoid acting shocked or looking down on him/her, because of their language, dress, or lifestyle choices.
• Ask her if she feels in danger.

To report a possible victim or to get help, call the National Human Trafficking Hotline at 1-888-373-7888 or text BeFree to 233733.

Adapted from www.hopeforjustice.org and www.polarisproject.com.

WHY DON'T THEY LEAVE?

The women and children under a pimp's control will often not self-identify as victims of sex trafficking or seek help on their own. The following is a list of common reasons why victims of domestic sex trafficking cannot or will not leave their exploitative situations:

CAPTIVITY / CONFINEMENT
→ Locked indoors, locked in rooms, or locked in closets.
→ Interactions are monitored or controlled by the sex trafficker (i.e., pimp).

USE OF VIOLENCE
→ Severe physical retaliation (beatings, rapes, sexual assault).
→ Threats against loved ones.

SHAME
→ Humiliated by the activities they have been forced to perform.
→ Brainwashed by the pimp to blame themselves.

DEPENDENCY / LOYALTY
→ Relying on the pimp after years of control.
→ May have a debt to the pimp that they feel they need to pay off.
→ Stockholm syndrome similar to Battered Women's Syndrome.

ISOLATION

→ Unfamiliar with surroundings due to frequent movement.
→ No personal ID or documentation which is often confiscated by the pimp.

DISTRUST

→ Brainwashed to fear law enforcement by the pimp or learned distrust of law enforcement due to direct negative experiences.
→ Have been told lies or deceitful information

HOPELESSNESS

→ Resigned to the "fact" that they'll never get our of their situation.
→ Feelings of no self-worth, disassociation, giving up, and apathy.
→ May not understand social service infrastructure or how and where to access help.

Adapted from "Domestic Sex Trafficking: The Criminal Operations of the American Pimp" (The Polaris Project - www.polarisproject.org)

31 WAYS to TAKE ACTION

Knowledge without action is of little help to those who are suffering in your city. While not everyone will take up the issue of sex trafficking in America as his or her "cause", we know that many will want (and need) to respond in practical ways. That's why we've assembled a list of possible action steps for individuals, groups, or entire churches/organizations.

PROMOTE AWARENESS & AID PREVENTION

1. **Host a screening of IN PLAIN SIGHT** at your home, school, workplace, or church, and use this Group Study Guide. More info: www.inplainsightfilm.com/screening

2. **Educate yourself, friends, and family** about sex trafficking in the United States by visiting the Polaris Project website for more information – http://bit.ly/USsextrafficking.

3. **Host an information session** and invite a qualified speaker.

4. **Post news stories** about sex trafficking on social media.

5. **Hang posters** with the National Human Trafficking Hotline number (888-3737-888) at motels, restaurants, and restroom stalls. Download the poster at http://bit.ly/sextraffickinghotline.

6. **Form a neighborhood watch group** or educate your homeowners association on what indicators neighbors should be looking for and how to report.

7. **Speak out to local retailers** when they offer products or advertising that glamorize pimping or sexualize children.

END DEMAND

8. **Affirm upstanding men in your community** who exemplify moral conduct and honor women and children with their words and actions.

9. **Discontinue using porn.** If you view pornography, there is a high probability that you will eventually seek to purchase sex. We would encourage you take steps to develop healthy relationships and seek help to recover from this habit / addiction. More info: www.xxxchurch.com

10. **Stop purchasing sex.** If you are buying sex, please know that women or children don't enjoy being with you. They fake the experience, because they'll be beaten if they don't bring back enough money or accumulate enough money to support their drug addiction. Please consider getting support and developing healthy relationships through programs like Celebrate Recovery or Sexaholics Anonymous. To find a group in your area, visit www.celebraterecovery.com or www.sa.org.

11. **Mentor young men.** Introduce the "Empowering Young Men to End Sexual Exploitation" curriculum for high school boys at your local schools in order to educate young men about the harms of prostitution and to enlist them as allies in the movement to end violence against women and girls. More info: www.caase.org/prevention

12. **Attend local zoning hearings**, and speak up when someone wants to bring questionable businesses into your community.

ADVOCATE FOR LEGISLATIVE CHANGE

13. **Learn what laws exist** at the city, county, and state levels, and start to understand any deficiencies. Make your voice known to lawmakers, and vote accordingly.

14. **Write or call your local judges and county officials** to encourage them to educate themselves on the issues of sex trafficking, and send them a copy of the IN PLAIN SIGHT documentary.

MAKE A PERSONAL IMPACT

15. **Recognize the signs** that someone may be a victim of sex trafficking – http://bit.ly/signsoftrafficking.

16. **Report suspicious activity** to 911 or the National Human Trafficking Hotline at 888-373-7888.

17. **Invest in the lives of your children** and teaching them that all human beings are to be loved and valued.

18. **Treat women as equal members of society,** and avoid turning women into objects (objectifying) through your thoughts, words, and actions.

19. **Discontinue using the term "prostitute" or "ho"** – understanding that a woman is being prostituted or is prostituting herself. Her identity and value are so much more than being sold for sex.

20. **Discontinue using the term "pimp" or "pimpin" in a positive light** – understanding that there is nothing glamorous or honorable about coercing, manipulating, or forcing a woman to have sex for money.

21. **Give generously** to one of the six non-profits featured in the film that run aftercare homes and fight against sex trafficking – www.inplainsightfilm.com/donate

22. **Dedicate your gift giving** to include products made by survivors or benefitting organizations that are fighting against sex trafficking in the United States. Examples include:
www.penhlenh.com
www.isanctuary.org
www.thistlefarms.org
http://store.nightlightinternational.com

23. **Become a foster parent**, and provide a loving foster home for a child.

HELP YOUR CHURCH MAKE AN IMPACT

24. **Host a prayer event** using an existing prayer guide specifically focused on trafficking. Resources: http://bit.ly/guidetoprayer

25. **Host a fundraiser or benefit concert** for a non-profit that runs an aftercare home and fights against sex trafficking. Recommended organizations: www.hopeforjustice.org

26. **Support educational and vocational programs** in your area for at-risk girls.

27. **Approach your local juvenile justice system** about presenting "Traps of a Trafficker" to female minors on a regular basis. More Info: http://bit.ly/trapsofatrafficker

28. **Start a Celebrate Recovery or support group** for men and women struggling with porn or sex addiction. For more info: www.celebraterecovery.com

29. **Compile a list of counselors in your area** that specialize helping men and women with porn or sex addiction, and have it ready to refer to people as needed.

30. **Host a "Porn and Pancakes" men's event** - a morning filled with straight talk about porn and the issues surrounding porn, from the people who get it. More Info: http://bit.ly/pornandpancakes

31. **Prayerfully consider opening a licensed aftercare home** for survivors of sex trafficking.

HYMN LYRICS

To help fund the work of Hope for Justice, an accompanying music album is available for purchase and features hymns recorded by well-known artists who turn our attention to the hope and healing needed to overcome this darkness. We hope you'll utilize the songs in a time of weekly worship as you gather with your small group.

In Christ Alone - Natalie Grant

In Christ alone my hope is found
He is my light, my strength, my song
This Cornerstone, this solid ground
Firm through the fiercest drought and storm

What heights of love, what depths of peace
When fears are stilled, when strivings cease
My Comforter, my All in All
Here in the love of Christ I stand

In Christ alone, who took on flesh
Fullness of God in helpless Babe
This gift of love and righteousness
Scorned by the ones He came to save

Til on that cross as Jesus died
The wrath of God was satisfied
For every sin on Him was laid
Here in the death of Christ I live, I live

There in the ground His body lay
Light of the world by darkness slain
Then bursting forth in glorious Day
Up from the grave He rose again

And as He stands in victory
Sins curse has lost its grip on me
For I am His and He is mine
Bought with the precious blood of Christ

No guilt in life, no fear in death
This is the power of Christ in me
From a lifes first cry to final breath
Jesus commands my destiny

No power of hell, no scheme of man
Could ever pluck me from His hand
Til He returns or calls me home
Here in the power of Christ I stand

I will stand, I will stand
All other ground is sinking sand
All other ground, all other ground
Is sinking sand, is sinking sand
So I stand

It is Well - Jeremy Camp

When peace like a river attended my way
When sorrow like sea billows roll
Whatever my lot, Thou has taught me to say
It is well, it is well with my soul

It is well with my soul
It is well, it is well with my soul

My sin, oh, the bliss of this glorious thoughts
My sin not in part but the whole
A nail to the cross and I'll bear them no more
Praise the Lord, praise the Lord, oh, my soul

It is well with my soul
It is well, it is well with my soul

We sing holy, holy, holy, we sing holy, holy, holy
And we sing holy is Your name, oh, most high (x2)

And Lord please haste the day when my faith shall be sight
The clouds be rolled back as a scroll
The trumpets shall resound and the Lord shall descend
Even so it is well with my soul

It is well with my soul
It is well, it is well with my soul (x2)

Grace That Is Greater - Building 429

Search me, O God, and know my every thought
Discern my every way and speak into my soul
Point out to me, my wrongs, convict me
Until I follow down the path that leads me to Your will

Because my heart, sometimes, can wander
And my faith, at times, can stray
But I know that when I fix my eyes on You
That I will always remain safe in the shadows

Of Your grace, grace, Gods grace
Grace that will pardon and cleanse within
Grace, grace, Gods grace
A grace that is greater than all my sin

I praise You because I'm fearfully made
You formed my frame in a secret place
All of my days, ordained before I breathed
Written in Your book before I came to be

Because Your love, I stand and wonder
You know I come to Thee
And knowing that when I fix my eyes on You
I will always remain safe in the shadows

Of Your grace, grace, Gods grace
Grace that will pardon and cleanse within
Grace, grace, Gods grace
A grace that is greater than all my sin

A grace that is greater than all my sin
It's greater, it's greater, greater than all my sin
It's greater, it's greater, it's greater than all my sin
It's greater, it's greater, greater than all my sin
It's greater, it's greater, greater than all my sin

Nothing But the Blood - All Sons and Daughters

What can wash away my sin?
Nothing but the blood of Jesus;
What can make me whole again?
Nothing but the blood of Jesus.

Oh! precious is the flow
That makes me white as snow;
No other fount I know,
Nothing but the blood of Jesus.

Nothing can for sin atone,
Nothing but the blood of Jesus;
Naught of good that I have done,
Nothing but the blood of Jesus.

Oh! precious is the flow
That makes me white as snow;
No other fount I know,
Nothing but the blood of Jesus.

This is all my hope and peace,
Nothing but the blood of Jesus;
This is all my righteousness,
Nothing but the blood of Jesus.

Oh! precious is the flow
That makes me white as snow;
No other fount I know,
Nothing but the blood of Jesus.

Oh! precious is the flow
That makes me white as snow;
No other fount I know,
Nothing but the blood of Jesus.

Just a Closer Walk With Thee - Bart Millard (Mercy Me)

Daily walking close to Thee,
Let it be, dear Lord, let it be.

Just a closer walk with Thee,
Grant it Jesus, is my plea.
Daily walking close to Thee,
Let it be, dear Lord, let it be.

I am weak, but You art strong;
Jesus, keep me from all wrong;
I'll be satisfied as long
As I walk, let me walk close to Thee.

Just a closer walk with Thee,
Grant it Jesus, is my plea.
Daily walking close to Thee,
Let it be, dear Lord, let it be.

When my feeble life is o'er,
Time for me will be no more;
Guide me gently, safely o'er
To Thy shore, dear Lord, to Thy shore.
To Thy shore, dear Lord, to Thy shore.

Just a closer walk with Thee,
Grant it Jesus, is my plea.
Daily walking close to Thee,
Let it be, dear Lord, let it be.
Let it be, dear Lord, let it be.

Trust And Obey - Big Daddy Weave

When we walk with the Lord
In the light of His word
What a glory He sheds on our way
While we do His good will
He abides with us still
And with all who will trust and obey

Trust and obey, For there's no other way
To be happy in Jesus, But to trust and obey

But we never can prove
The delights of His love
Until all on the altar we lay
For the favor He shows
For the joy He bestows
Are for them who will trust and obey

Trust and obey, For there's no other way
To be happy in Jesus, But to trust and obey

Lord, I love You
Please help me to trust and obey
Lord, I love You
Please help me to trust and obey

Then in fellowship sweet
We will sit at His feet
Or we'll walk by His side in the way
What He says we will do
Where He sends we will go
Never fear, only trust and obey

Trust and obey, For there's no other way
To be happy in Jesus, But to trust and obey

Trust and obey, For there's no other way
To be happy in Jesus, But to trust and obey

Lord, I love You
Please help me to trust and obey
Lord, I love You
Please help me to trust and obey
Lord, I love You
Please help me to trust and obey

The Sound That Saved Us All - Anthony Skinner

All hail the power of Jesus' name
Let angels prostrate fall
Bring forth the royal diadem
And crown him, crown him, crown him Lord of all

I just want to sing Amazing Grace
How sweet the sound that saved us all

Let every kindred tribe
On this here terrestrial ball
To Him all majesty ascribe
Crown him crown him Lord of all

I just want to sing Amazing Grace
How sweet the sound that saved us all

Oh, with that yonder throng
That we too at his feet may fall
And join the everlasting song
Crown him, crown him crown him Lord of all

I just want to sing Amazing Grace
How sweet the sound that saved us all

How Great Thou Art - The Digital Age

O Lord my God, When I in awesome wonder,
Consider all the worlds Thy Hands have made;
I see the stars, I hear the rolling thunder,
Thy power throughout the universe displayed.

Then sings my soul, My Saviour God, to Thee,
How great Thou art, How great Thou art.
Then sings my soul, My Saviour God, to Thee,
How great Thou art, How great Thou art!

And when I think, that God, His Son not sparing;
Sent Him to die, I scarce can take it in;
That on the Cross, my burden gladly bearing,
He bled and died to take away my sin.

Then sings my soul, My Saviour God, to Thee,
How great Thou art, How great Thou art.
Then sings my soul, My Saviour God, to Thee,
How great Thou art, How great Thou art!

When Christ shall come, with shout of acclamation,
And take me home, what joy shall fill my heart.
Then I shall bow, in humble adoration,
And then proclaim: "My God, how great you are!"

Then sings my soul, My Saviour God, to Thee,
How great Thou art, How great Thou art.
Then sings my soul, My Saviour God, to Thee,
How great Thou art, How great Thou art!
How great Thou art, How great Thou art!

Be Thou My Vision - Fernando Ortega

Be Thou my vision, oh Lord of my heart
Naught be all else to me, save that Thou art
Thou my best thought by day or by night
Waking more sleeping, Thy presence my light

Be Thou my wisdom, and Thou my true word
I ever with Thee and Thou with me Lord
Thou my Great Father and I Thy true son
Thou in me dwelling and I with Thee one

Riches I heed not, nor man's empty praise
Thou mine inheritance, now and always
Thou and Thou only, first in my heart
High King of Heaven, my Treasure Thou art

High King of Heaven, my victory won
May I reach heaven's joys, oh bright heaven's sun
Part of my young heart, whatever befall
Still be my vision, oh Ruler of all

Come Thou Fount Of Every Blessing - Mark Schultz

Come Thou fount of every blessing
Tune my heart to sing Thy praise
Streams of mercy never ceasing
Call for songs of loudest praise

Teach me some melodious sonnet
Sung by Flaming Tongues above
Praise His name, I'm fixed upon it
Name of God's redeeming love

Hitherto Thy love has blessed me
Thou has brought me to this place
And I know Thy hand will bring me
Safely home by Thy good grace

Jesus saw me when a stranger
Wandering from the fold of God
He to rescue me from danger
Bought me with His precious blood

Oh, to grace how great a debtor
Daily I'm constrained to be
Let Thy goodness like a fetter
Bind my wandering heart to Thee

Prone to wander, Lord, I feel it
Prone to leave the God I love
Here's my heart, oh, take and seal it
Seal it for Thy courts above
Here's my heart, oh, take and seal it
Seal it for Thy courts above

Rock of Ages - Page CXVI

Rock of Ages, cleft for me, Let me hide myself in Thee.
Let the water and the blood, From Thy wounded side which flowed.
Be of sin the double cure. Save from wrath and make me pure.

Not the labor of my hands, Can fulfill Thy law's demands;
Could my zeal no respite know, Could my tears forever flow,
All for sin could not atone; Thou must save, and Thou alone

Nothing in my hand I bring, Simply to the cross I cling.
Naked, come to Thee for dress; Helpless look to Thee for grace.
Foul, I to the fountain fly; Wash me, Savior, or I die.

Wash me, Savior, or I die
Wash me, Savior, or I die
Wash me, wash me, Savior, or I die
Wash me, Savior, or I die

Rock of Ages, cleft for me,
Let me hide myself in Thee.
Wash me, Savior, or I die.

Great is Thy Faithfulness - Elijah Young

Great is Thy faithfulness, O God my Father;
There is no shadow of turning with Thee;
Thou changest not, Thy compassions, they fail not;
As Thou hast been, Thou forever will be.

Pardon for sin and a peace that endureth
Thine own dear presence to cheer and to guide;
Strength for today and bright hope for tomorrow,
Blessings all mine, with ten thousand beside!

You are so faithful even when
I've turned my own way
Your loves so deep, it covers me, endures always

Great is Thy faithfulness, O God my Father;
There is no shadow of turning with Thee;
Thou changest not, Thy compassions, they fail not;
As Thou hast been, Thou forever will be.

FEATURED ORGANIZATIONS

We hope the IN PLAIN SIGHT documentary educates you on the issue of sex trafficking in the United States and motivates you to take action. We are honored to feature six fully-vetted, trustworthy organizations in the film, and **we invite you to support their work financially** by making a donation directly through their website.

HOPE FOR JUSTICE
Stacia Freeman - U.S. Director (Nashville, TN)
www.hopeforjustice.org

COURAGE WORLDWIDE
Jenny Williamson - Founder (Sacramento, CA)
www.courageworldwide.org

P.A.T.H - PARTNERS AGAINST TRAFFICKING HUMANS
Louise Allison - Founder (Little Rock, AR)
www.pathsaves.org

REDEEMED MINISTRIES
Bobbie Mark - Co-founder (Houston, TX)
www.redeemedministries.com

THE SAMARITAN WOMEN
Jeanne Allert - Founder (Baltimore, MD)
www.thesamaritanwomen.org

TRAFFICK911
Deena Graves - Founder (Dallas, TX)
www.traffick911.com

WHO TO SUPPORT?

When evaluating aftercare homes to support (beyond the six featured in the IN PLAIN SIGHT documentary), we encourage you to ask these types of questions. Good intentions are not enough. Professionalism and accountability are critical when working with survivors of sex trafficking.

→ Does the program include trauma-informed counseling by a licensed professional?

→ Is the identity of each child/woman kept confidential?

→ Are minors used to fundraise for the organization?

→ Are females and males housed on completely separate properties?

→ Is the facility licensed so there is accountability for policies and procedures?

→ Do those working and volunteering for the facility have to undergo a stringent vetting process?

→ Is the location undisclosed?

JOIN THE MOVEMENT

1. HOST A SCREENING

For more information on how to host a screening of the IN PLAIN SIGHT documentary in your area, go to **www.inplainsightfilm.com/screening**.

2. SUPPORT AFTERCARE HOMES

To make a donation directly to one of the organizations featured in the documentary, go to **www.inplainsightfilm.com/donate**.

3. SUPPORT THE FILM

To make a tax-deductible donation to Awaken Media and help us spread the film across the world, go to **www.storiesoffreedom.com**.